RACHEL WILSON is a writer and the founder of The Grief Network, a community run by and for bereaved young people. Her writing has appeared in *The Times*, the *Guardian*, the *New Statesman* and more. She is currently training to become a barrister.

Praise for *Losing Young*:

'Incredibly refreshing'

FLORA GILL, *The Times*

'Well-researched and engagingly written, covering everything from sex after grief, how mourning is approached differently throughout the world and returning to work after loss. A must-read for anyone wanting to understand their own grief better, feel less alone – or even learn more about this important part of life more generally'　　　PRUDENCE WADE, *Independent*

'Examining grief through this particular lens, as well as discussing how to navigate the complexities of partying, and dating, when you're in grief, Wilson's book will make young grievers feel seen'　　　*The Standard*

'Beautifully written'　　　PANDORA SYKES

'Thoughtfully and beautifully written, but most important of all, an incredibly useful take on facing grief as a young person'
CARIAD LLOYD, author of *You Are Not Alone*
and host of *Griefcast*

'A brilliantly, brilliantly written exploration of young grief. Endlessly absorbing, it is packed with clarity, curiosity and courage'

FELIX WHITE, guitarist for The Maccabees
and author of *It's Always Summer Somewhere*

'The truth is, it has turned on so many lights for me that I had to read slowly, carefully and with space to reflect. I've met familiar ideas I didn't know I carried, I've had assumptions challenged and anxieties assuaged. I feel I've attended a masterclass about supporting my bereaved friends, taught by a kind and patient expert speaking with love from the heart of her loss ... What a profoundly helpful book'

KATHRYN MANNIX, author of *With the End in Mind* and *Listen*

'Twentysomething loss has been largely and notably overlooked in bereavement books for the past few decades. No more! *Losing Young* is a welcome and necessary addition to the field. And Rachel Wilson is a bright new voice'

HOPE EDELMAN, author of *Motherless Daughters*
and *The AfterGrief*

'An important and insightful book about the loneliness of grief and the transformative power of community'

GAVANNDRA HODGE, author of *The Consequences of Love*

'As an educationalist, I have seen far too many children lose parents and others dear to them. This book is full of wisdom and compassion and will help many far and wide'

ANTHONY SELDON

LOSING YOUNG

How to Grieve When Your Life is Just Beginning

Rachel Wilson

WILLIAM
COLLINS

William Collins
An imprint of HarperCollins*Publishers*
1 London Bridge Street
London SE1 9GF

WilliamCollinsBooks.com

HarperCollins*Publishers*
Macken House, 39/40 Mayor Street Upper
Dublin 1, D01 C9W8, Ireland

First published in Great Britain in 2023 by William Collins
This William Collins paperback edition published in 2024

1

A catalogue record for this book is
available from the British Library

ISBN 978-0-00-850810-4

Set in Dante MT Std
Printed and bound in the UK using 100%
renewable electricity at CPI Group (UK) Ltd

MIX
Paper | Supporting
responsible forestry
FSC
www.fsc.org   FSC™ C007454

This book contains FSC™ certified paper and other controlled
sources to ensure responsible forest management.

For more information visit: www.harpercollins.co.uk/green

To James and Dad

Contents

Introduction

The morning I found out my mother was dying I was horrifically hungover. I'd just finished my finals for my master's degree and I'd been out the night before celebrating in one of the tiny underground clubs in Bath, whose walls were permanently coated with sweat. It was May. I was looking forward to the summer, my dissertation the only thing standing in the way of me leaving this tiny but beautiful Georgian city. It had felt suffocatingly small since I had arrived there from Melbourne, where I had lived and worked for two years previously. A couple of months before my finals, my boyfriend had dumped me over the phone from Australia. Shortly after, I celebrated my twenty-fifth birthday. I felt bereft that I had reached this perfect mid-twenties mark with only false starts to show for it. I was still waiting for my life to begin.

I was riffing on this typical quarter-life crisis tale as I complained to a friend on the phone that morning, lying on the sofa, unshowered, in my underwear and a T-shirt, trying to ignore the waves of nausea that were rising from my stomach to my throat. We were speaking about Berlin, a city where he'd lived, and where I was determined to move after I finished my dissertation. To me, it held all the promise of a European Melbourne, with the benefit of being much cheaper, much closer to home and having much bigger clubs. My parents were exasperated by this idea (*What's wrong with the UK?*). My restlessness made me seem, to them, directionless at best, work-shy and complacent at worst. That appraisal was echoed in the media. It was 2017 and Millennials were the lightning-rod generation for age-old cavils about young people. We just needed to quit moaning and get a better job. None of the difficulties we faced were actually real.

When I hung up, I saw that I'd received a text from my dad. He and Mum wanted to come to visit for the day. That was strange; they would usually meticulously plan their visits, driving down for when my favourite café opened at 8 a.m. I'd meet them there, sleepy and almost always late. I can still picture them in their habitual corner spot, my dad reading a newspaper, my mum playing on her phone with her reading glasses on. She would jump out of her seat with her arms stretched wide open to grip me into an aggressive, loving hug when she saw me. This new spontaneity of visiting mid-afternoon was odd. My gut stirred, but I brushed it aside as the churning stomach of someone who'd drunk too much beer the night before. I lifted myself from the sofa and got in the shower, trying to pretend that everything was normal.

When you tell a story, the presumption is that it's complete – that it ends. Narration shapes events and gives them meaning. The master's I had completed was in translation. I spent hours each week picking apart language, fine-combing various registers of French and German texts, angsting over nuance and meaning. I read the theories on transposition and modulation, meaning loss and how to mitigate it. But loss, the theory warned me, was always inevitable. That's how it feels to write about grief. I can write about the beginning, the middle and the end of my mother's illness. I can write about her death. Yet in giving it form or linearity, I will give you something inaccurate. If there is a 'beginning' to the story of my grief, it would likely be that day in Bath when I was told my mother was ill. She had been diagnosed with cancer for the third time in her life.

What I didn't know then was that grief begins at diagnosis. That insight came when I spoke to the bestselling author and leading grief therapist Julia Samuel, sometime after my mother died. It suddenly made sense of that year when my mother was ill. I still moved to Berlin as planned, in the blind hope that we had time, and because she wanted me and my brother to continue living our lives. There, I did my best to adhere to what I thought it should look like for a twenty-something to live in Berlin. From the outside, I succeeded. I functioned like any other young person: I still went out drinking, to clubs, to work; hooked up with people; woke up hungover; listened to podcasts; went on holiday; posted on Instagram; complained about work, about politics, about my salary. On the inside, I was in turmoil. I couldn't work out why I wasn't having fun, why I wasn't falling in love with Berlin the way I had fallen for Melbourne. I slept poorly, washing sleeping pills down with wine or smoking the joints my friends rolled at bars to override the terrifying loop of death-oriented thoughts that would consume me when my head hit the pillow. If I didn't, I would cry so hard that the physical pain would make it difficult for me to breathe and I would wake feeling more shattered than I did after staying out at a club until dawn. During the day, I would find myself physically holding my breath or chewing the inside of my mouth on the U-Bahn in the morning. My shoulders were perma-tensed up towards my neck and my stomach would be gripped, as if anticipating a punch in the gut. My body was responding to the violent fear of losing my mother, but my mind rarely connected the dots. I didn't realise I was already grieving.

Neither did anyone else. My friends in Berlin didn't know my mother was ill. My close friends from home visited me occasionally and would tell me I was 'coping really well' but that I could tell them 'if I ever needed anything'. I had no clue what I needed. We'd continue to talk about all the things we'd always spoken about: crap boyfriends or dating-app ghosters, shitty jobs and patronising bosses, tear-inducing rents and mouldy walls. We'd talk about our futures and the things we hoped lay there. Yet I was no longer present in these conversations. A deep schism had opened between us: I felt like I was spectating my friends' problems – concerns I'd related to only weeks before – from a strange position, off-centre, wildly off-axis. Time progressed but my perception of it helixed erratically between anticipating an unrelentingly dark future and the relative warmth and stability of the past. The future was no longer something that held promise, no longer something I wanted to plunge headlong into. It was bleak: when I tried to imagine what my life looked like without my mother in it, I couldn't. It turned up black, like a dead computer screen. What made it worse was that I knew no one else my age who had been through it – who might be able to paint a picture of how that blackness could come to be reilluminated.

My mother died the day after my twenty-sixth birthday, in April 2018, just a year after she was diagnosed. I received the call to come home on a Thursday night in late March. Berlin was experiencing a freak cold snap. I sat, rocking, on a bench outside a bar, hood pulled over my head, as snow fell gently around me, coating everything in soft white. I flew home. I was by her side as she died, with my father and my brother, sometime near dawn. We arranged the funeral. In the weeks that followed, I braced myself for the wave of grief to crash. It never did. I was already at sea.

*

During the weeks leading up to her death, my mother said something to me that would change the course of my grief. She suggested that, after her death, I find a support group for young people.

Instinctively, I knew this was what I craved. If I could talk to someone else who had been through it, they could tell me what to expect: how the loss might change me, and what grief would feel like, at this age. By the same token, I felt an aversion to being among middle-aged people who'd lost older parents – parents who'd had the chance to watch their children grow up, get married, have children of their own. They'd had so much more time. What I was experiencing was different.* I didn't

---

* As I will reiterate throughout this book, when I contrast younger adults with 'mature' adults and contend that they have different or distinct experiences of grief, I am *not* arguing that one is any better or worse, more or less painful, than the other. Nor am I arguing that they are *absolutely* distinct; as we will see, there are elements to grief that are universal.

want to be made to feel even worse, or even more alone. But when I searched online for a young person's grief group, I couldn't find any. There were groups for children, but of course I wasn't a child. The rest lumped 'adults' together generically. I was angry that there was nothing separate for younger adults; it seemed so obvious to me that it was needed.

Three days after my mother died, in hopes of finding a young person's grief group, I wrote in to one of my favourite podcasts – one I knew had lots of other twenty-something listeners. It was called *The High Low*, a Millennial-focused pop-culture and news podcast that was enormously popular, accumulating 30 million downloads in the four years it ran, before it folded in 2020. The hosts read out my email, asking if any listeners knew of any young person's grief groups, during an episode that happened to air on the day of my mother's funeral. The hosts told me they received a 'deluge' of responses; they forwarded nearly 200 emails to my inbox in the following days.

'When I listened to your last episode, I nearly crashed my car. Everything she said was like hearing my own thoughts from when I lost my mum aged 20 ...'

'The letter you read out about the girl who lost her mum made me burst into tears on the Tube. I don't know of any groups for millennials but I'd love to share my experiences with her if it helps ...'

'There just aren't any groups that an 18–30-year-old who has lost a parent can really feel a part of ...'

Glued to my phone reading these emails, I felt I had struck a wellspring of young grief. The responses – many of them written in long paragraphs, offering advice and solace – pierced the very lonely bubble I felt trapped in. For the first time, I knew I wasn't an anomaly. I knew I wasn't alone. Even more remarkably, I felt the first glimmers of relief and reassurance. Many of the respondents offered to meet up with me. I began to meet young people all over London who had experienced bereavement in their late teens and twenties, all with different relationships to the deceased and all at different stages down the line. Soon after, I hosted a group meet-up in a pub in East London on a hot summer's evening. It was like the world's weirdest blind date. Making small talk was difficult when we all knew that asking, 'So, what brings you here?' was essentially asking, 'So, who died?' I could sense the nervousness in the room and I myself had felt apprehensive about the meeting. Yet as introductions were made and the conversation began to flow, the atmosphere shifted. When I looked around the room, I realised there was a levity to it. Relief. People were laughing, animated, in deep conversation. The group stayed until last orders, many lingering outside afterwards, exchanging numbers under the light of the streetlamps overhead. One girl, who'd lost her father seven years before, emailed me the next day. She nearly hadn't come, she said, but 'it was incredible to meet such strong, courageous people. What I really took away from the evening was that, looking around the room, there wasn't a tear in sight. It was just a lot of "OMG, you too?" or "I dealt with it like that as well!"'

That was the beginning of The Grief Network, as I came to name it. At pubs across London, we often looked like a birthday party, or someone's leaving do. Once, a woman asked us if we were a singles event. Another evening, with the blackest of ironies, we realised a wake was being held next to us in the pub. Countless times, new attendees would approach me to tell me how they nearly hadn't come. What they'd imagined was a bleak and sad affair, and they weren't sure how they would cope with talking about their person's death. The meetings defied their expectations. It wasn't sad or morose. It was just kind of like hanging out with mates at the pub. It helped to talk about how you were feeling. It could even be kind of fun. In those meetings, young people were finally having the chance to articulate the distinct challenges they were facing to others who understood. They could talk about what it was like getting through your first break-up without your mother to comfort you; struggling to assert your need for time off work after your father had taken his life; having to make funeral arrangements and pay household bills for your parents as they grieved the loss of your sibling. They could talk about their unexpectedly crap friends and surprisingly supportive co-workers; how they'd cried at their best friend's wedding or birthday; how they'd developed a reliance on drugs, drinking and sex – or (more often) how those hedonistic things healed them, connecting them back to other people and making them feel their age again.

This was all in contrast to the difficulty of navigating grief with their friends. Often among mates, young grievers felt grief was a kind of conversational bombshell: something that killed the mood and prompted awkward silences. It was a topic they learnt to tiptoe around. Talking to other grievers at meet-ups helped them to articulate better the emotions they were feeling, which, in turn, helped them to talk to their non-bereaved friends about their grief. That reciprocity helped, too, in understanding that the things they had worried were abnormal, or were them not grieving 'properly', were in fact common – that other people had felt, responded, reacted or behaved in the same ways that they had. All the silent chastisement or fears they had experienced over the years went away. As one young man I spoke to put it: 'Everything I'd thought was wrong or strange about what I'd felt was validated. I wasn't failing at grieving, I was just normal.'

'My mum died when I was 26.' I've now uttered this sentence, or some version of it, countless times in five years. Sometimes I deliberately say I was 25 because it feels emotionally accurate, even if factually untrue. So much is contained within those seven words – an ongoing story that many assume, upon hearing me speak them, is complete. Much of what is contained in those words is completely unique to me and the relationship I had with my mother – an experience I felt I was completely alone in. I have come to learn, though, that as unique as my grief was and is, it is also in many ways typical. So many of my feelings, my behaviours, my difficulties are things that other young people have had to navigate in their own ongoing stories of grief. It has only been through the exchange of those stories that I have grown more comfortable, more accepting of my grief. When once I thought I stood alone in a room, I now know I stand there among many.

One

Quarter-life Grief

Running Grief Network meet-ups, it quickly became clear to me that my instincts had been right: 'quarter-life grief', falling at this transitional stage of life between adolescence and adulthood, came with distinct challenges and characteristics. To add to those challenges, young people felt that they were not recognised by existing support services; that their distinct challenges were not acknowledged. I had faced so many of them myself as that 25-year-old whose world was torn apart by her mother's diagnosis. So why, at the time of my mother's death, was a group for young grievers not available? What are the characteristics of what I colloquially refer to as 'quarter-life grief'? And why had quarter-life grief not been recognised as a distinct bereavement experience before? To answer those questions, we must look at how grief is conceptualised in our society more generally, and how it came to be so poorly and broadly misunderstood.

I harboured those misunderstandings myself. Before my mother became ill, I believed grief was just an intense form of sadness. I thought that this simple emotion would subside with time, through the famous 'five stages' (see pages 19–21), with no understanding of how grief might continue to feature in one's life more materially. To the extent that I assumed it was just an internal emotion, that grief was something that happened privately, cocooned within the family of the deceased. It might be intrusive to ask a bereaved person about the person they were grieving for and it would certainly be upsetting to ask them how they were feeling. The bereaved should simply be left to deal with their grief *on their own*.

When my mother was diagnosed, I realised slowly that the assumptions I held were wrong. I expected to know instinctively how to react and behave, as though someone might pass me a 'young person with a dying mum' playbook. Of course, there was no such thing and the lack of guidance or knowledge of how grief might manifest made me constantly question my choices. I often worried I wasn't 'doing it right', something that continued to concern me after my mother died. These misconceptions weren't derived from nowhere. If I felt I was play-acting at being an adult as I dealt with my mother's illness, I realised I'd also had a strange expectation of being handed a script. You know that character; you've seen them on the television. It's the troubled youth who turns to drugs to mask the pain. It's the young woman who wears too much make-up and sleeps around because she just wants to feel something. It's the person who screams and falls to the floor of the supermarket when they get the call. It's the noble-looking talking heads on war documentaries, the director making heroism out of trauma.

Death and mourning have become taboo in our culture over the last century. These universal features of human life have such limited expression, politically, socially and culturally, that many of us arrive at our first major bereavement near totally grief illiterate, harbouring all the misconceptions that proliferate in the space that lacuna leaves. We didn't always suffer from this cultural ankyloglossia around grief. It is an inexorable and inextricable part of being human. In *The Anatomy of Grief*, Dorothy Holinger, a psychotherapist who spent 20 years working at Harvard Medical School, charts the emergence of rituals around death and grief. While grief-like responses have been widely observed in many animals, humans are unique in our ritualisation and memorialisation surrounding the dead. This begins with the act of burial, early evidence of which dates back to our ancestors, the hominids, 400,000 years ago. 'It was at this point in our evolutionary history that death became both real and abstract,' writes Holinger. In our ability to conceptualise death, we also contemplated what happened to the deceased *after* death, which became the founding beliefs in human religion. Being able to hold our dead *in mind* in fact coincided with the development of our frontal lobe in the brain. This unique ability to continue to ideate our dead explains how grief is expressed both *intrinsically*, through the constellation of emotions we experience when someone we love dies, and *extrinsically*, through our culture, the rites, prescriptions and prohibitions we develop.

While the emotions of grief can be felt universally, the 'how' of our grief varies from culture to culture. Each society or religion will have its own norms and rules around the 'proper' length of mourning, the responsibilities and roles of the family members left behind, and what constitutes 'acceptable' behaviours in terms of processing grief. As bestselling author and grief coach Hope Edelman observes, how we mourn tends to be 'an outgrowth of [our] culture's belief system'. In many systems, grief is decidedly collective and the rules surrounding it reflect this. In Aboriginal culture, for example, the norms of 'sorry business' include the tradition of not uttering the name of the deceased, which, in modern times, extends to not writing or printing their name either, or producing pictures of them. Speaking the name of the deceased is said to disturb their soul, so substitute names are used instead for a period of time. Speaking to the online Aboriginal cultural resource Creative Spirits, Aunty Margaret Parker of the Punjima people in Western Australia describes sorry business as a cultural practice that embeds the individual's death in the wider community: 'The family belongs to us all. The whole community gets together and shares that sorrow. It don't have to be close family. We share our grief by crying and that's how we break [it], by sharing together as a community.'

In Tana Toraja, in the South Sulawesi province of Indonesia, the dead are periodically unburied during the Ma'nene festival. Favoured ancestors' corpses are cleansed, dressed and walked around the village, allowing small children to meet their dead relatives sometimes for the first time. Even before burial has occurred, the body is preserved for months at home, during which time it is still fed and cuddled. Over 8,000 kilometres away, Madagascans practice '*famadihana*' for up to seven years after their relatives' deaths. Otherwise known as 'dancing with the dead', it involves exhuming the bones of the dead, rewrapping them in fresh shrouds and re-sealing the crypt ceremonially. In Mexico, the renowned Día de los Muertos festival is an occasion of celebration for people to pay respects to deceased friends and family members. In the Jewish tradition, mourners are guided through the first year of grief (*shnat ha-evel*) from the moment between death and burial (*aninut*) to the first week after the funeral (*shiva*) and beyond.

As with most human rituals and festivals, these practices are necessarily communal in nature. They encompass a much longer timeline for mourning and, in so doing, recognise the extended length of grieving. In contrast, Edelman observes, 'In modern, individualistic, Protestant-influenced societies like the United States and the United Kingdom, the social component of bereavement rarely extends beyond the funeral and burial services.' To other societies, the idea that our social interaction would end after the funeral would clearly be anathema. They certainly wouldn't countenance giving the recently bereaved a wide social berth and avoiding mentioning the death at all, as has become a norm in Western societies. On a few occasions after my mother's death, I would meet up with friends I hadn't seen in a while and tell them about her passing. At that moment, they would look at their toes and sheepishly admit that they knew but hadn't known what to say.

How did the West become so alienated from our deeply human need to externalise grief, socially if not collectively? It is a largely modern phenomenon. In the Middle Ages in Europe, a 'good death' was a public one. According to Joëlle Rollo-Koster at the University of Rhode Island, medieval Europeans' idea of the 'perfect' death was a long, slow decline that allowed the dying and the bereaved to perform acts of contrition, prayer, confession and absolution, and to prepare for the afterlife. Cemeteries were social locations, sometimes even used as markets, or places to gamble and drink. 'Images of death abounded,' writes Rollo-Koster. 'It was part of life, ritualized and choreographed – unlike today where it is hidden and closeted.' Over the centuries, our cultural image of death evolved but it became no less culturally visible: in the Romantic era, death and grief were expressed in a stylistic, overtly emotional manner, depicted in literature and art as highly aestheticised and valorised. If modern society asks mourners to 'get over' a death, the Romantics vilified those perceived to have moved on too quickly after the death of a loved one.

Grief reaches its cultural apex in Victorian times. The era of 'high mourning' largely ushered in by Queen Victoria's lifelong expression of grief at the loss of her husband is where most of our modern funerary traditions derive from. Elaborate rites and regulations were developed, their performance mostly falling to upper- and middle-class women. Dresses were dyed black or grey to signal whether the family were in 'deep' or 'half' mourning respectively. In a complex tariff, the length of time these periods lasted depended on the relative: a widow was expected to be in deep mourning for her late husband for two years, while a parent who had lost a child would be in deep mourning for a year. The funeral industry blossomed as ceremonies became more expensive, monuments more ostentatious.

Of course, not all mourning rites – from whatever society – are universally welcome. Grievers whose culture prescribes celebration may wish they could sit alone in peace to nurse the sorrow they feel. Those in cultures that dictate sombre mourning may wish they could express gratitude and joy about the deceased's life. Virginia Woolf described the atmosphere in her family home after her mother's death, when Woolf was 13, as 'a muffled dulness [sic]', her family 'sad, solemn, unreal, under a haze of heavy emotion'. Edelman, following the Jewish ritual of *shiva* after her mother's death, talks about her disconnect from the rites in an otherwise non-observant family ('I'd just turned seventeen. It seemed archaic and unnecessarily complicated to me.'). Yet many grievers I have spoken to wish that we still had some way to publicly convey our grief, like the black Victorian dresses, so that strangers would treat them with kindness when they forgot what they were doing in a shop or were moving too slowly in rush hour on the Tube.

The decline of Victorian 'high mourning' culture began as war raged through Europe at the turn of the century. Thanks to a policy of non-repatriation, First World War soldiers were fated to rest where they fell on foreign soil; for their families, there were no deathbed goodbyes, no funeral processions and no burials. With unprecedented numbers of deaths under traumatic circumstances, many families repressed their grief. With 116,000 dead in the US, 900,000 dead in the UK and 1.4 million in France, few in these societies were left untouched; the academic Adrian Gregory has estimated that around 3 million Britons lost a close relative, son or brother, while the secondary bereaved who mourned a cousin, friend or neighbour 'encompassed virtually the entire population'. Mass mourning laid thick over the nation in post-war society and new rites were created. In Westminster Abbey, in Arlington in the States and under the Arc de Triomphe in Paris, the body of one unknown soldier came to represent all; one grave had to inter hundreds of thousands of dead in each nation.

Armistice Day was conceived to memorialise the nation's loss. It aggrandised senseless death into acts of heroism and bravery, and respected sacrifice, but did little to represent the everyday, infinitesimal pains of grief. While pomp and ceremony required respects to be paid silently, veterans suffering 'shell shock' (PTSD) ended up homeless in parks in London, and an inquiry into shell shock found that men who continued to be tormented by it were simply too cowardly to overcome it. Individual grief was minimised because a loved one's death could only ever be one among many – a drop in an ocean of unspeakable death. And death did become unspeakable. All of us who have given remembrance with two minutes of silence know that oppressive quiet; I remember the gravity of Remembrance Day as a child, trying with all my might to remain uncannily still and quiet, learning that this was how you dealt with tragedy. Public commemoration equates grieving with silence; that to honour something difficult, we must not speak. It's a public enactment that teaches us from a young age that the language of bereavement is a wordless one; that the ritual of remembrance is mute. We do not enquire and we do not keen; we keep quiet and carry on.

It was not just the wars. The Spanish flu pandemic of 1918, much as the coronavirus pandemic has done in recent years, affected funerals, meaning they were very small or cancelled altogether. Mourning periods contracted. The scale of death meant that families and communities were experiencing multiple bereavements. If the Victorian 'deep mourning' timelines were followed, they would simply never get a break from grieving. Hope Edelman also notes that women's emancipation played a role: as many of the rituals of grief fell to women, with their newfound liberties they were no longer willing to bear the sole responsibility of the austere and oppressive rules of high mourning. At the same time, faith in religion was declining and medical interventions were increasing. Our lifespans were getting longer and the 'afterlife' was not a driving idea in people's lives anymore. Urbanisation disconnected people from their families and communities, meaning the 'nuclear' or immediate family were more relied upon for support rather than the wider community. This perfect cocktail resulted in the privatisation, isolation and stigmatisation of grief and death. By the mid-twentieth century, the notion that we ought to move on from or get over a loved one's death had become more prevalent.

The modern warping of grief was further entrenched by the pathologisation of bereavement. Writing just before the First World War broke out, psychoanalyst Sigmund Freud produced a theory of grief in *Mourning and Melancholia*, published in 1917. Freud delineates between a 'normal' response to grief, which he deems to be finite and naturally processable, and longer, depressive responses to bereavement. It is from *Mourning and Melancholia* that grief was first conceptualised as 'work' (*Trauerarbeit*), the corollary being that the successful completion of this work would result in the griever detaching from the deceased. This 'severing ties' model is the origin of modern notions that grievers should mourn in short order and 'get over' or 'move on' from the death. Critiquing this harmful notion, Hope Edelman writes: '[Freud's] theory was a good fit for an industrial, capitalistic economy, as it promised to guide workers out of grief and back to their labours quickly and with minimal disruption to productivity.' Mourning behaviours that did not follow this linear model, but which had previously existed on a spectrum of acceptable responses, 'acquired labels such as "pathological", "excessive", "chronic", "delayed", "suppressed"' and so on.

Fast-forward half a century and the seductive myth of grief linearity found new form in the most famous bereavement model: the five stages of grief. You know the ones: denial, anger, bargaining, depression and acceptance. I remember learning about them when I was a teenager; in fact, it was my mother who told me about them. These neat five phases hail from the groundbreaking work of pioneering psychiatrist Elisabeth Kübler-Ross, set out in her book *On Death and Dying* in 1969. Kübler-Ross worked with terminally ill patients in an era when it was still the norm to keep the patient ignorant of their prognosis. When they were told, however, they would move through five distinct stages as death approached – an observation that is still relevant for those who are terminally ill today. But the five stages also quickly became misapplied to grief, an experience they were never intended to describe. This neat progression to a place of acceptance was picked up by the media and took on a life of its own, despite Kübler-Ross's protestations. In many of the interviews included in this book, young grievers questioned where they were in the stages or raised the possibility that they hadn't progressed far enough through them. The misapplication of Kübler-Ross's model can be a powerful root cause of grievers thinking they are grieving 'incorrectly' or 'unsuccessfully'.

It is easy to see why we have become so seduced by the five stages of grief. Five phases seem manageable; it suggests a journey you can passively travel through, awaiting the golden destination of acceptance, where everything will feel better again. You'll no longer feel the sharp heat of anger at the injustice of your person's death. You'll no longer feel the tug of quicksand that is depression. You won't lie awake all night wondering, *If only we'd caught the cancer earlier. If only she hadn't taken the car that day. If only I'd known he was feeling that way.* Five is a manageable number: it's the days of a working week; it's the acts of a Shakespeare play. You can count them on just one hand. The problem is that trying to apply five neat stages to grief is like trying to fit a constellation in a photo frame: ill-fitting, diminishing and impossible. Grief is altogether more expansive, more three-dimensional, more enduring, than a five-bullet checklist.

Believing that we can 'complete' grief has harmed innumerable people over decades. As award-winning *Griefcast* host Cariad Lloyd writes in her book *You Are Not Alone*, the rage she felt after her father died when she was 15 was all-encompassing. Looking at the 'map' of the five stages, she began to feel ashamed that she could not experience any of the other waypoints: 'How could I get to this magical land of Acceptance if I hadn't completed all the levels? I hadn't even beaten the big boss in Anger yet. How many gold coins did I have to collect before I could leave Depression?'

Academics have long doubted and debunked the 'five stages' model, even as it remains a modern mainstream myth. Towards the end of the twentieth-century, psychologists and academics recognised that the 'severing ties' model of grief, compounded by the five stages, left the bereaved feeling as though they'd failed in their task of grieving if they could not, in fact, 'cut' the deceased from their lives. It was, in fact, a study that focused on children that re-illuminated the knowledge we had so long lost: that our natural, human impulse is to continue to memorialise our dead, long after they die. The groundbreaking 1996 Harvard Child Bereavement Study collected data via interviews with children who had lost a parent, as well as talking to the surviving parent, over a period of two years after the death. The researchers found that children intuitively continued to foster a relationship with the deceased parent: 81 per cent felt their parent was 'watching over' them, while 77 per cent kept and cherished a personal belonging of their parent's. That did not mean they were under the false impression that the parent was still alive or would return. The children were in fact 'constructing' the dead parent by continuing to invoke memories of the parent, and engaging in behaviours that helped them cope with their absence. Significantly, so was the surviving parent. These findings were articulated in the 'continuing bonds' model of grief, where the bereaved is most helped by continuing to foster a relationship with the deceased. Charting the course of these psychological 'discoveries', Hope Edelman, in her immensely helpful book *The AfterGrief*, questions whether there was anything special about those children and parents in 1992 – were they doing anything different to mourners 40, 50, 60 years earlier, by staying connected to the dead? She concludes that the findings were a reflection of the loosening of strict taboos around grief and death: 'Maintaining inner relationships with lost loved ones wasn't a new development. Mourners had been doing it all along. They'd just been doing it quietly and privately, to avoid being told they were grieving wrong.' Turns out our early ancestors – and millennia of human culture – had it right all along.

Defining Quarter-life Grief

This is the culture quarter-life grievers find themselves in. The discussion in this book about their specific needs and the way services are currently underserving them is just one problem to be solved within a larger reimagining of the way we resource, prioritise or contemplate bereavement on a social, cultural and political level. Arriving at my first significant bereavement at the age of 25, I was woefully ill-equipped to grieve, as were many of the other quarter-life grievers I subsequently met. There were emotions and experiences we shared with all bereaved people, but we also each believed we were facing problems more closely related to our stage of life.

'The thing about grief is: it throws you into a completely alien landscape,' leading grief expert and Founder Patron of Child Bereavement UK Julia Samuel explains to me. 'So when you're young, at a time of your life where you already feel uncertain, it heightens that feeling of "I don't know where I am, I don't know where I'm going. I don't even know *who* I am. My birth certificate says I'm an adult, but I don't feel like one." Research shows now that you're not really an adult until you're 28, 30. At 25, you wanted more of your mum to help see you through to when you could really feel like a grown-up. You wanted your mum to help sort you out,' she tells me.

'Your mum's death was a death out of time,' she continues. 'She didn't have her expected lifespan, so you felt robbed of her, but also of a future you felt you had a right to. All the images you had of her in your life – of her being at your wedding, the birth of your baby – all those significant events in your life that she won't be present for.' That's why I was so turned off by the idea of a generic adult support group. 'If you're in a room full of people who haven't shared that same experience, you feel misunderstood, and it misshapes how you feel on the inside. You feel angrier. If you're in a group of 50-year-old women whose mothers had died, say, you'd be thinking: "Fuck off, I don't know what you're crying about. You got 20, 30 years more than me."*

---

* To reiterate: it is not my argument that being bereaved young is 'worse', or being bereaved as an older adult is not painful. The kinds of comparisons Samuel talks of are an expression of the negative emotions of rage or resentment that are common to grievers of any experience. It takes the rational and calm brain to remember and acknowledge that *everyone's* experience of the loss of someone significant in their life is painful and valid.

I know my mother felt this injustice, too. In the weeks before she died, she lay on the sofa and I tried to think of all the questions I might want to ask her. As we spoke, she sighed and looked away, as if irritated. 'I'm disappointed,' she said. 'You should have had me for 30, 40 more years.'

As Samuel alludes to, psychologists have now redefined the age of maturing from 18 to 25. In the UK, this means those in their early and mid-twenties are entitled to access a child psychologist. Developmentally, you are not classed as an adult, even if you are legally. This tracks with recent developments in how we understand the 'emerging adulthood' years of independence, famously identified and articulated by psychology Jeffrey Arnett at the turn of the millennium.[1] Roughly defined as lasting from 18 to 29 years old,[2] emerging adulthood, as summarised by Arnett, is an age of identity formation and instability.[3] The characteristics associated with emerging adults are those that have now become popularly associated with Millennials, and now with Gen Z, too,* in the Western cultural conscience. Arnett describes this period as marked by identity explorations and flexibility that can also be experienced as instability. As young people are either priced out of or choosing to delay the traditional markers of adulthood such as marriage, home ownership and parenthood, they instead inhabit an 'in between' existence that is not quite adolescent or truly adult. In this period, emerging adults have no normative roles that they

---

* The utility and rigour of generational 'science' has been questioned, with one view being that named generations have little use beyond that of a marketing tool – and an imprecise one at that. I use these generational labels for ease of reference and because of some of their cultural relevance, without wanting to over-emphasise the perceived generational wars that the media are fond of.

need to play (parent, manager, spouse), and are typically financially and residentially unstable. 'It is only in the transition from emerging adulthood into young adulthood in the late twenties that the diversity narrows and instability eases, as young people make more enduring choices in love and work.'[4] In terms of self-perception, emerging adults do not see themselves as teenagers or grown-ups. To paraphrase the icon Britney Spears, emerging adulthood is when you are not a child, not yet an adult.

Typical milestones such as marriage and children are not seen as the true markers of adulthood. Instead, for this demographic, financial independence and the attendant self-sufficiency it brings are a key marker. Adulthood is seen as accepting responsibility for oneself and making independent decisions. The upside to all this? Young people can explore their identity, mixing up their aspirations in love, work and their values in the world. Love during emerging adulthood is typically experienced as deeper and more intimate than relationships arising in adolescence, while work experiences become more focused towards building longer-term careers than the summer jobs of the teen years. An emerging adult will explore new world views and re-examine notions they have been taught as teenagers and children, normally through their higher education or early work experiences. The downside of this flexibility is the feeling of flux and a lack of control: these are the underlying emotions that score the stereotypical 'quarter-life crisis' narrative, with which I was so familiar at 25, finishing my master's and hoping direction would come of it.

In the 20 years since Arnett first published his study, there are yet more concerning trends for young people. It is well documented that Millennials are getting married and having children later than any other generation previously, while being on track to be the first generation to be financially worse off than their parents. Gen Z, generally taken to be born between 1995 and 2009, report higher levels of poor mental health than any other generation has before, in reaction to the greater political, environmental and economic instability of our era. They are likely to overtake Millennials as the least- or latest-married[5] and reproductive[6] generation yet. With social media now ubiquitous and woven near-inextricably from young people's lives, its effects on mental health are of growing concern. A Pew Research Center study found that, although a significant number of teens thought social media positively fostered connection and contact, 24 per cent thought social media had a mostly negative effect, with 17 per cent feeling that platforms such as Instagram and TikTok harm relationships and result in less meaningful human interactions. Young people are now the demographic most at risk of experiencing loneliness, and happiness among UK young people has hit a 13-year low with 35 per cent of 16–25-year-olds saying they have never felt more alone.[7]

Grief is an isolating experience for anyone. If you are already feeling alone, destabilised and disconnected, that isolation becomes more acute. In one of my visits home from Berlin, I remember sitting in the kitchen with my mum. She held me as I cried, and I told her: 'I just feel so *alone*.' Though isolation is a common feeling for any mourner, statistically speaking it's an accurate one for young grievers. According to the US Census Bureau, the percentage of people experiencing the loss of a parent in late adolescence (15–19) is under 5 per cent. By the age of 29, this is still just shy of 10 per cent for father-loss and under 5 per cent for mother-loss. Only as you reach your late forties does father-loss become more statistically likely than not, while mother-loss only becomes so in your mid-fifties (see graph below). In the UK, a Child Bereavement UK survey found that 7 per cent of British adults had been bereaved of a parent or a sibling when they were a child.[8] That's equivalent to one child in every average class. Imagine being that one child, surrounded by 28 other people who cannot begin to fathom what you feel or how you must adapt.

What is the impact of all this isolation – emotional, statistical or otherwise? The research on emerging-adulthood bereavement is scant, reflecting the lack of bereavement services specifically catered towards this demographic. But from the studies performed so far, the death of a significant person in early adulthood emerges as a potentially life- and identity-changing event, at a time when a young adult's sense of

Percentage of People With Deceased Parents By Sex of Parent

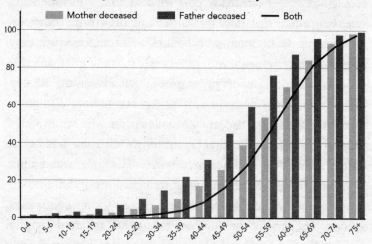

Graph from the U.S. Census Bureau, Survey of Income and Program Participation, 2014 Panel, Wave 1.

self is in flux.[9] It puts emerging adults at risk of long-term maladaptive coping strategies,[10] including a heightened risk of depressive symptoms, low self-esteem and life dissatisfaction.[11] In a 2021 study authored by Shannen Jones and Matteo Martini of the University of East London,[12] there was found to be a relationship between a weak sense of self and the incidence of depression in bereaved emerging adults. Those in the study were also found to have poorly adapted to their grief following the death of their parent. The study authors suggested that interventions for bereaved emerging adults, such as support groups, should aid them in building a stronger sense of self by helping them to rebuild their identity following a loss. For the young griever, the death cleaves life in two: there is the 'you' before they died, and the 'you' after they died. This feeling is often summed up when young grievers say: *When they died, a part of me died with them.*

A small American study published in 2021 concluded that emerging adults may need specialised support groups addressing their unique developmental challenges.[13] The demographic 'need opportunities to engage with others experiencing grief, and may benefit from specialized support groups that address the developmental challenges inherent among this population.' I spoke to one of the authors of this study, Natalie Porter, who set up a grief support group for students at her university when she was a graduate student. She lost her own father when she was young. 'Speaking from experience, I went to a grief group full of older people and they really wanted to *go there*. They don't wanna mess around. They're not there to have fun. When I started my own group, the young people who came wanted to have fun. They didn't wanna just go to this group every week and sit there and cry. They wanted to be able to freely talk about their loss or not talk about their loss with other people who they knew had experienced something similar but have fun at the same time.'

This is what I experienced when I gathered those young grievers together in the pub on a summer's night in East London. At that first meet-up, there were deep conversations, but there was also laughter and new friendships blossoming. That night, many of us for the first time got to embody two parts of our identity at the same time: bereaved, but still young. 'Being able to voice and share the grieving of a future you expected with other people who are missing that too is healing,' says Samuel when I ask her if she thinks more support groups for young people should exist. 'Because it affirms. One of the most difficult things about grief is that it's invisible and that you feel alienated and isolated anyway, and so it's the connection to others that helps you manage it. Being with people your own age takes the resentment and the rage out of it – so with that completely taken out of your internal landscape, you're cleaner and clearer to hear each other, more compassionate, more empathic to yourself, and the people around you.'

Hope Edelman told me that, in the course of running her own motherless-daughter grief retreats, she had recognised the need to hold retreats specifically aimed at women who'd experienced loss in their twenties. 'We identified that transitional period of life as significant enough to have a special retreat just for those women, and it filled very quickly to capacity. They were very grateful that we were acknowledging that, in their twenties, they still really had one foot in the family and one foot out the door.'

So, how do we define 'quarter-life' grief? My attempt at a loose (and necessarily general) definition would be:

A grief precipitated by the death of a significant person which **cataclysmically disrupts your assumptive world**. Your expectations of life – the images you held of that person, in the life you thought you'd live – are drastically and indefinitely altered. The road you assumed you were on has forked irrevocably and you're now on a new track that you cannot get off. This disruption happens **at a time in your life when your world is already unstable**: your identity is in flux; you do not enjoy financial, domestic, social or professional stability. For other people your age, that instability is a flexibility that can be enjoyed, explored and exploited. For you, it becomes a source of anxiety, anger or fear. Grief therefore becomes part of your *formative* **experience**. It shapes your identity, your decisions and your adulthood: you feel forced into an accelerated maturity, but you may also experience a sense that part of yourself is fixed at the age the loss occurred, making it difficult to adopt a fully adult sense of self. Your identity **diverges**: there is the 'you' before grief, and the 'you' after. You can never not know that the worst thing might happen, so your brain operates off this knowledge in a way that those of your peers do not. In that way, you feel **isolated: the disruption is one that is not relatable to others your age**. They are less likely to have their own experiences of loss to draw from to help support you, leaving you either unsupported or unrecognised. As you grow and develop following the loss, you may experience a greater sense of **resilience and perspective** that sets you apart from other people your age. But it can also manifest as a continued **anxiety and fear** throughout life of the same thing happening again, to other people you love or to yourself. Finally, this is something you live with **for the rest of your life**. If you live your full life expectancy (currently 80.9 years in the UK), a loss at 25 versus 55 means you are living with grief for the majority of your life, rather than the minority. In that time, it has the potential to interact with every milestone you move through – every change, good or bad.

Before we progress any further, some necessary caveats. Acknowledgement is a major part of grief, so here are some of mine. Youth is not the *only* defining feature of a young person's grief. It is not the only factor that is relevant. To borrow from the work of leading critical race theorist Kimberlé Williams Crenshaw, there is an intersectionality in grief. As explored, a person's grief will bear the marks not only of their internal emotional landscape, but their historical context. It is therefore also informed by their race or diaspora culture, their sexual and gender identity, their class, their disability, and other identity factors. It will also be informed by the relationship to the deceased: parent/parent-figure, sibling/ sibling-figure, aunt, uncle, friend, partner, ex, grandparent, pet. The type of death is also a major factor: if it was sudden, slow, due to illness, an accident, suicide, murder. If the death was traumatic, the grief is more likely to be complex, intense and hard to express.

I have also talked about our 'cultural heritage', in my case being the predominant culture of the UK and other Western countries like it. Not everyone will relate to this predominant culture or feel it to be relevant to their intimate experience of grief. In Britain, there are plenty of people whose families form part of the diaspora of other cultures, which will have a far greater impact on how they grieve or the norms of mourning as they understand them. However, even those from diaspora cultures will come into contact with emanations of the dominant culture when they navigate and interact with bereavement services, medical services, counselling services, educational institutions, workplaces and the administrative process around death, both in the private and public sector. In those environments, they are at risk of being treated insensitively or discriminatively. This raises the need for culturally sensitive and literate bereavement support and palliative care.

In writing this book, I have aimed to talk to young people with myriad experiences. I have aimed to represent different identities, types of deaths and relationships to the deceased. I will not have succeeded in portraying *all* experiences. Many of the people I spoke to lost parents. Others lost siblings, friends, boyfriends. In neglecting to write about, for example, the death of a grandparent or the death of an aunt, a godparent, a parent-in-law and so on, I do not mean to diminish or disenfranchise those griefs. I have not covered spousal loss, or child or pregnancy loss. These can, of course, happen when one is young, but I see them as distinct experiences in and of themselves, which deserve a more dedicated enquiry than this book can do justice to. Even if I have spoken to someone whose grief matches, to some degree, your own, you may feel that my conception of what it is to be young is misguided or wrong. If you have picked up this book in the hope of feeling seen or heard, and it does not give you that, I can only apologise and lend my voice, as I do, to the calls for more numerous and more diverse representations of bereavement, young or otherwise, in all its kaleidoscopic colours.

Finally, I have trained my lens most intensely on young people today. This is not to suggest that people of older generations who lost someone significant did not experience the difficulties of 'young grief'. After writing a piece about my experience, I received many emails from older readers who talked about what a relief it was to hear something that resonated so much with their experience of loss dating back 20, 30, 40 years. They wanted to give me advice on living my life to the fullest, but also expressed regret that nothing like The Grief Network existed when they were younger. They had lived a long time feeling alone in what they experienced and had faced multiple instances of being misunderstood in the meantime. (One emailer who lost her sister when she was 22 wrote to tell me that a friend of hers had lost her sibling much later in life. The friend told Emailer that her grief was probably worse and more painful because she'd had her sibling around for much longer, so had more memories to grieve. Needless to say, Emailer cut contact with the 'friend'.)

So, let's return, once again, to that summer's evening in London, 2018. Picture that room full of young people, all dealing with their own brutal and exquisitely human griefs, both completely unique and at the same time shared with the others surrounding them. They are talking about their hopes, their fears, their anger, their sadness; how confused they have been, how alone, how anxious. They are talking about the changes they have felt in themselves and their lives, both good and bad. They are talking about all the milestones they wished they could have shared with their person, and the ones yet to come.

Step into the room. Let's make some introductions.

Two

Leavers

Leaving school, going on the lash and gaining independence

Mia was one of the listeners who heard my plea for help being read out on *The High Low* podcast. She wrote an email describing the death of her mother when she was 18, when all her friends were concerned about was organising a boozy holiday and she was still a 'stroppy teenager' her mother would never live to see grow up. I replied to Mia and soon we were meeting for breakfast on a warm day in June, nearly three months after my mother's death. She asked how I was doing in the way that someone does when they expect your honest answer to be a long one. I replied in the way I did in the early days, giving a pragmatic and frank assessment of the situation and dwelling on the awful details of my mother's physical decline. It helped to be given room to talk about the particular devastation of watching the body of some-one you love deteriorate and shut down.

Mia could relate. Her mother had also died of cancer. She listened intently and empathetically, but I was acutely aware that Mia had been much younger than me when her mother died. Between the ages of 18 and 26, so many 'firsts' happen. Before the cancer that killed her, my mother had suffered the disease twice before, once when I was 11 and once when I was 17. At 17, I was miserable: I hated school, my early romances were fraught and I didn't have strong friendships. I had no idea how to be myself and all I wanted to do was fast-forward to my future as quickly as possible. My mother recovered from the cancer; she lived to see me go to university, meet my first long-term boyfriend and get my first job. I tried to convey to Mia that I knew a gap existed between us; that we shared so much but we had also experienced things differently. I didn't want her to think that I thought what we had been through was exactly the same, the way I didn't like older people talking to me about their parents' deaths as if we were peers.

If Mia felt any resentment, she didn't show it. She was warm and funny, and told raucous stories about her student days and messy nights at awards ceremonies and events in her job as a publicist. I told her about the coke-habit posh boy I had started seeing whose friends kept managing to bring up parents in substance-fuelled conversations, forcing me to limber uncomfortably around my mother's very recent absence in an environment I'd sought out to try to forget about it. Mia told me about the ups and downs of an on–off thing she'd been having with a boy she'd known for years from university. We spoke of the difficulty of balancing the wish to 'be young' and have a good time with the heavier weight of grief. I told Mia I wanted to organise a meeting for the other young, bereaved people who'd emailed me, and she helped book the pub that would host that very first meet-up. She has been at the heart of The Grief Network ever since.

Eighteen is the legal age of adulthood in the UK. It is the canonical moment when your driving licence magically transforms into a passport to pubs, clubs, credit cards and the voting booth. It is the age many of us leave school and head off to university, a formative time of newfound autonomy, when drinking, drugs and dancing can offer escapism. It may be hedonistic, scary, complicated – all and any of the above – but it is the time when you're least likely to expect your life to collapse because someone close to you has died. I wanted to ask Mia what it was like to lose her mother at that symbolic age, teetering between childhood and independence.

When I first met Mia, she was six years into her grief. When I sit down to talk to her for this book, she has just passed the ten-year anniversary of her mother's death. Her mother was diagnosed with cancer when Mia was two, passing in and out of remission through Mia's life. Her mum having cancer was Mia's perpetual norm. 'When they're sick for a long time, you think they will just be sick forever and it will be fine,' she says. But in her last year of sixth form, Mia's mother started to display troubling symptoms. A family friend, who was a nurse, told Mia and her father to take her mother to a doctor. She was admitted to hospital on Christmas Day in 2012.

Mia recalls herself being a 'moody teenager' who thought nothing of her mother's condition at the time. 'Mum loved to sing and loved Christmas, so she made us sing Christmas carols on the ward. I remember being *so* embarrassed – like, *Oh my God, why are we singing?*' Everything happened quickly. 'It was just after Christmas. All my family started showing up and I was *very* unamused. Why was Aunty Claire here from Norfolk?

What was my godmother doing, booking a flight from Sydney? A couple of days before New Year's Eve, Mum's doctor took me and my dad into a room and said, *Your mother might die*. My dad started crying, which was weird because he never cried. I just thought, *Well, no, because she hasn't died for 18 years, so why would she die now?* I was very much in denial.'

On New Year's Eve, Mia was supposed to be going to a party. She was looking forward to it; a boy she fancied was going to be there and it was the perfect opportunity for her to hook up with him. But early in the morning, Mia's family received a call from the hospital telling them to come in. By the time they arrived, Mia's mother had died. 'I remember being just … Even though she had been sick for so long, I was in such shock.' The family stayed in the hospital room, crying, talking and spending time with her mother's body.

'After we left and the initial shock had worn off, I remember thinking, *Oh shit … now I can't go to the New Year's Eve party!*' Mia laughs. 'I wanted to get with that boy and I remember thinking I'd have to tell someone I wouldn't be there.' The day wore on and as the evening came, Mia and her cousins decided to go to the local pub to get out of the family house and give her father time to be on his own. Sitting in the busy pub surrounded by people gearing up to celebrate New Year, Mia suddenly decided she still wanted to go to the party. She felt awkward about being at home, she felt awkward around her father's tears, and she didn't know how to handle her wider family's careful attentiveness. Although her cousins tried to dissuade her, Mia called a friend, who met her at the pub and took her to the party. 'I remember I was wearing UGGs and a Hollister cardigan. All the other girls were in dresses and heels. A friend saw me and asked why I was wearing what I was wearing. And I just said, "Oh, my mum died today." He looked at me, like, *Why are you here?* And I was like, "I don't know!"'

Mia managed to have fun at the party. She kissed the boy that she fancied. She stayed out all night and convinced her family she was sleeping over at a friend's house. She enjoyed the possibility of being out and having a good time, even though she knew she had so much to cope with when she eventually came home. Her behaviour that night illustrates the divide young grievers face, torn between two worlds: the 'normality' that their peers continue to enjoy and experience, and their new internal landscape, one destabilised by grief. Balancing these two realities was something Mia had to contend with as she went on the boozy school-leavers holiday to Magaluf with her friends, then on to university and eventually into her first job.

'I stopped revising for my A levels. I had been a pretty good teenager, but I started to go out drinking all the time, and going to all the parties I could. Because I was 18, people just thought I was so fun.' As a fresher, the hedonistic drinking culture at university further enabled Mia to bury her grief. 'Everyone drinks at uni,' she says, 'but for me, I didn't have a healthy outlook or relationship with anything or anyone. I slept with a lot of people. I hung around with people I shouldn't have. I didn't have a very nice time and I wasn't very happy. But it was the first year of uni – you're supposed to be drinking all the time. I had no concept that it was a mask for my grief.' Mia would find herself in 'sticky situations' and not know who to turn to. Drinking occasionally enabled her to express her emotions, albeit in ways her friends could not immediately understand. 'One time, I got so drunk and felt so sad, I just threw all the mugs in our student house at the wall. Dad had to come and plaster over the damage. It seems obvious now that it was an expression of grief that I wasn't facing, but no one around me at that age really understood it beyond me being a bit mad and strange. Sometimes I wish I could go back and explain it to them.'

Was she conscious of her grief at all? 'Yeah, I thought about Mum a lot.' Reflecting on her time at university and the 'messiness' of it, Mia wonders how different things might have been with her mother still there to give her advice. They had a close relationship. 'We always did things together. She was a really embarrassing mum. She wore really bright clothes; she loved to sing, bounce around. She played guitar. She was an art therapist and played piano. She was a social worker at a rehabilitation centre. She'd take me in and explain [that] the people she helped had had a tough life and that was why they were in the position they were in, and I was lucky because I'd had better choices available to me. She grew up in Australia and was always very affected by the history and tensions between the white population and Indigenous people, so I think she was always trying to give back and make up for it in society. She was very loving and she always wanted to be involved. I could tell her things; she knew I'd started having sex with my school boyfriend, but Dad didn't. She'd tease me by telling me I had to ask Dad if I could go and stay at my boyfriend's house. She picked me up from there once and I had a love bite. Dad asked what it was and she told him I'd burnt my neck with my straighteners.'

Even though Mia felt herself getting to an age where she was putting more distance between herself and her mother, she still missed having her guidance. 'I maybe would have gone to a uni that was further away, and maybe I wouldn't have gotten into those sticky situations where I wanted her advice in the first place. I think we'd have still been in regular contact. I would think about what she'd think of the boyfriends I had, or what she would have thought about me graduating. I was doing so many things for the first time: cooking, budgeting, navigating new friendships. Dad tried his best. My cousins tried, too. But it wasn't the same as Mum. There wasn't really any advice left available to me. I had to figure things out on my own.'

I ask Mia if she thinks the drinking and wildness were a crutch. Was it something she turned to because she had no other support? The answer is more complex than a simple yes or no. On the one hand, Mia describes how her friends were not emotionally attuned to her needs. 'Lots of them were clearly very awkward around it or had a *pull yourself together* attitude.' Her school boyfriend was no better. 'Mum had told me to break up with him and enjoy being young and explore, so I did break up with him. But when she died, he made it all about him and said, *I lost someone, too*. As in, my mum. He was one of the people who told me I should be staying close to my dad instead of going off to uni. There wasn't much in his response that was really about me.'

Mia may not have had much support around her, but she didn't seek it out or accept people's attempts either. 'It was 2012. The conversation about mental health just didn't exist then. I didn't speak to anyone. Dad had the more all-consuming grief and I felt very awkward around it. I think I gave the grief to him. I was happy for him to be the centre of it. When my godmother came over recently from Australia – she's amazing; she voice-notes me all the time and she's a good connection back to Mum and her heritage – she said to me something about what an impact Mum's death must have had on me as a teenager. No one had *ever* said that to me before. I think I'd given it to Dad. If people asked me about Mum, I'd say "poor Dad". I wanted to get on with my life. My cousins tried to talk to me about it, but I was so self-conscious. When she died, I'd thrown myself onto one of my cousins, crying, and I was so embarrassed about that outburst. Dad would try to talk about it sometimes and I just didn't want to. It was mortifying. In some ways, I thought Mum wouldn't want us to be emotional or sad. And I hated seeing Dad cry. I didn't want to be helped, or to think about it. If people tried, I didn't want it. I pushed it away.'

This awkwardness manifested in her attitude towards the measures put in place to support her. When she returned to school after her mother's death, she was allowed to leave lessons – something she felt she took advantage of. 'I felt like I played it up, but at the same time, it wasn't as fun as I thought it might be when I'd imagined what life would be like if Mum died.' Mia felt this self-consciousness even when trying to engage with her grief. Her family scattered her mother's ashes in the Blue Mountains near Sydney, so she had nowhere she could 'talk' to her mother. She would visit the church at Guy's, the hospital where her mother had died, and wait for a dramatic moment to happen. She imagined bursting into tears and a stranger approaching her to ask what was wrong or console her. 'I was so inventive [coming up with] these TV-show situations that I didn't actually think about how I *was* feeling. As a teenager, you invent these moments because you're still figuring out who you are and what you want. But it's ironic because I didn't need to invent dramatic moments, because things were already pretty dramatic as they were!'

I ask Mia if now, at 28, she still uses drinking as a way of escaping her feelings. 'Not as much. I hadn't realised it was even a problem. I'd never stopped to think about it until we started doing The Grief Network. Meeting other people and hearing about their experiences made me realise I needed to think about all of it a bit more. You find others have had the same thoughts as you, the same guilt and doubt. I had always felt guilty about going to that New Year's Eve party. I was so focused on being 18, kissing the boy I liked, going to the party. But when I told other young grievers about it, they just nodded and were like, *Yeah, same*. They'd done similar things. I realised it wasn't bad. I didn't need to feel guilty anymore. I didn't need to judge myself. That played a massive part in me calming down, otherwise I think I'd still be running around doing stupid things at 28 now.' What has she learnt, ten years down the line? 'The ten-year anniversary was pretty bad. I was a mess for about six months before. On the day, I cried while my boyfriend was there. I don't talk about it with him that much, and always more pragmatically than emotionally. When I was crying I could see him think, *Oh my God! She's never cried before! Keep it coming!* He's much better at talking about emotions than me.' Despite the pain of that milestone, Mia talks about the more positive ways grief has shaped her. 'Few things faze me. As an older young person now, I see the qualities I wouldn't have had without grief. I'm independent, I'm calm. I feel like I know a lot about myself.' She admits that although she is an advocate of people getting therapy, she has never had it herself. She still feels scared of what might come up if she revisits her experience in depth.

After ten years, Mia says she has mostly adjusted to life without her mum. 'I think less about her, and more about the idea of her and what having a mother at this age would be like. I used to get so upset seeing mothers and daughters out and about. One time, I saw a woman on the Tube who had the exact same hands as Mum and I burst into tears. But I'm used to just having a dad now. I'm used to the relationship we have and the routine we have. When my boyfriend's parents met my dad, I wasn't sad that he had two parents there and I only had one. I'm very used to Dad having girlfriend drama. I'm used to hanging out with my mum's friends. I saw Mum's childhood best friend when she was visiting from Australia. She talked a bit about Mum. She said I was really like her, which was strange, because I don't know if I am. Because how would I know? I didn't get to know her as a person. Dad came with me, and he doesn't love being social so I was telling him, "Come on, Dad, stay for another ten minutes." Mum's friend said, "This is exactly what your mum used to do, too." I wouldn't know that, though.'

*

Mia's story strikingly shows how 'typical' young-person behaviours like going out and getting drunk can intermesh with grief, masking it while providing an outlet for it at the same time. Many people at meet-ups would report similar things: their reliance on partying to numb themselves or to avoid needing to confront feelings they found confusing and abnormal compared with their friends'. One young man I spoke to said he just simply had no idea what else to do. In excess, these behaviours are labelled as 'maladaptive' coping mechanisms – things that do more harm than good. They suppress the difficult emotions of grief and relieve the bereaved of having to face their feelings. The catch is that these feelings always find a way out in the end, and often in more painful ways than if a griever allowed themselves to feel the waves of pain as they crash. Numbing those feelings or distracting yourself from them never means you avoid grief; the more you push it to the side, the worse it feels when it eventually demands your attention.

No doubt, excess and avoidance are not great ways to process grief. We must, however, be careful not to overgeneralise and ignore the fact that young grievers still want to feel ... young. The stereotype of young people going off the rails is culturally prevalent. Think of the British phenomenon of *Skins* or *Fleabag*, or the American hit show *Euphoria*. I have never found these depictions hugely helpful. They normally focus too much on the dramatic spectacle of someone driven by unresolved pain, isolation and anger, without unpacking those feelings in any meaningful way. The 'hot mess' stereotype implies that going off the rails *is what grief looks like*. That's not true for *many* young people who find themselves carrying on as normal, while quietly falling apart on the inside, unable to communicate their needs. This can make them feel that they are doing grief 'wrong'. When my friends told me I was doing well, I was struck by the anxiety that because I wasn't outwardly a 'mess', they were completely missing the fact that my world was broken and fearful. I felt like I missed out on support because I wasn't puking my guts up or having a nervous breakdown. Portrayals that focus on the excess of drinking or drug taking don't help to unpack the experience of grief when the very behaviours they depict are those that are masking and obscuring the true feelings beneath.

There is also another side to the story. While some young grievers described themselves as a 'mess' – drinking excessively, hooking up with the wrong people, staying out all night – others found solace and healing in the exact same things. *Cosmopolitan* editor Catriona Innes writes about the loss of her mother in 2004, when she was 19. Innes was just a summer away from heading off to university, where she dreamed of dressing in vintage clothes, sleeping with boys and reading books on grassy lawns. Instead, her mother was diagnosed with a brain tumour, so she took up a job in her local Boots in Edinburgh. While she worked every day, her friends were off experiencing the life she had so looked forward to. She heard their heady university tales; they would call her from clubs, holding their phones in the air so she could hear the latest songs blasting from the speakers. Her existence was, in comparison, sad, and she felt life's promise 'drifting away'. A friend of a friend who worked as a barmaid saved her by getting her a job in the pub where she worked. There, Innes made a new group of friends whose lives looked like hers: working full-time, no university, living their lives independently. 'I was 19,' she writes. 'I didn't want to be the girl in a grubby white tabard, living a life of repetition and dead-behind-the-eyes dull sorrow. I wanted to *sparkle*.'

Her diary entries from the time reveal the quarter-life grief tension between frivolity and pain. 'They were an odd mix of love hearts (*Oh my god, he actually kissed me!*), glued-in club ticket stubs (*got soooo wasted last night, hehe*), and angry biro scrawls, some so full of fury they're practically illegible (*why the fuck do other people get to live, when she has to die?*)' Reflecting on her time as a barmaid, Innes cannot tell whether her grief drove her to drink more than she would have otherwise, or whether it allowed her to feel her age and shape for herself a life that was not completely consumed by death. 'When your mum is dying and you're drinking in the exact same way as everyone else is, what's toxic behaviour and what's normal behaviour becomes muddled. Very, very muddled. To the extent that I cannot untangle them, even today. The amount of alcohol I consumed would make me cry, something I rarely did during the day. I never said what I was crying for, although perhaps it was obvious. Instead, I blamed it on boys or losing a shoe. Living my life like the 19-year-old I was brought me so many slices of happiness during such a bleak time. Perhaps it wasn't destructive. Perhaps it was *needed*.'

Innes's experience chimes with another I heard from a young man I met at a meet-up. Ben, who identifies as queer and whose pronouns are he / they, told me about the judgement he felt when he went to Manchester Pride just days after his mother died of ALS (amyotrophic lateral sclerosis) when he was 24. He attended the event with his sister, and both siblings received messages from friends that questioned their decision to go. '"Shouldn't you be at home being sad?" was kind of the message,' he said. 'It wasn't concern, it wasn't, *Oh, are you feeling all right?* It was more that they obviously thought it was inappropriate because *their* expectation was I would stay at home, because that's what they imagined they would do if their mum died. And it was like, *Bitch! Your mum's not dead! So don't tell me how to act*.'

Ben spoke warmly of his mother's actions as an ally; she had been a huge support to him as a young queer man. 'I never had to come out, to her at least. She taught me to be myself. My sister was and is amazing for that, too. My dad's side of the family is Muslim, so that hasn't always been straightforward. So going to Pride, me and my sister *knew* Mum would have wanted us to go. She wanted us to feel joy, to live, and if she could have been there, she would have been. She was such a loving, sociable light of a person. She'd have hated staying at home and feeling sad. The woman never wore black a day in her life.'

Ben talked about how queer clubs provided the perfect space for him to feel something. 'I took my time. I still had days when

I didn't go out. I still had nights when I cried for a long time. I had those moments that people don't see on Instagram, so I was processing and trying to face up to it. But, fuck me, I also needed a break. I wanted to feel surrounded by love. I wanted to feel joy. Some of that joy was chemical and artificial as fuck, but it was a relief. It was the opposite of death, you know? It took the numbness away, allowed me to feel physically present. Mum would have loved me to take those moments of happiness where I found them.' Ben described queer spaces as those where people can work through their difficulties and still find respect. 'The gay community has so much grief intersected with it; people can be a bit more accepting that you're out to heal and work through pain by dancing all night and letting loose. I know that in itself is not just a "queer" thing, but for me, feeling part of a community helped to let it all out. But I was still doing the work when I was sober. I wrote a journal and talked to friends and I cried. I cried *a lot*. Partying just gave me the time off from that, [which] I needed, to reconnect to myself, to my friends, my world.'

I could relate to where Ben was coming from. The summer after my mother's death, I took time off work, travelled, went to music festivals and had a few messy nights out with friends. My mother wanted me to be happy. She wouldn't have wanted me to be laden with grief constantly. I had realised how short life could be; I was desperately trying to grab onto it where I could, when I spent so much of the rest of my time feeling adrift. Even the small pleasures of reading a book in the sunshine or ordering a curry and watching a favourite show with my best friend helped me have moments 'off' my grief. I wanted to learn to be kinder to myself, more caring, forgiving and encouraging, because those were the things my mother had done for me, and I needed to do them for myself now. Even before her death, long nights out in Berlin with friends could help alleviate the anxiety of anticipatory grief. I realised dancing until the cool grey dawns crept up on me meant that I had spent *hours* moving my body, often meditatively, in a trance to some body-consuming beat. Being out could be healing and make me feel like a normal twenty-something again.

These experiences track with Stroebe and Schut's modern 'dual process' grief model, which posits that grievers oscillate between cycles of grief orientation and recovery orientation.[1] Simply put, there are times when a griever just wants (and needs) time off from the task of grieving. Recent mourners must have an outlet for both phases: they need to spend time doing the 'work' of grief, and then they need a rest from it. For quarter-life grievers, the problem is distinguishing between when drinking and partying is a coping mechanism that is masking grief, and when it is actually a mechanism allowing them *time off from it*. When supporting young grievers, then, it is important (as it is with all bereaved people) not to jump to easy conclusions and put them in a 'coping' or 'not coping' box. It is certainly not acceptable to judge their responses and think that time off from grief – in whatever form that might take – is inappropriate or disrespectful.

It is, of course, a generalisation to tar all young people with the same brush of being myopically focused on drinking, shagging around and partying. Many buck this trend for a host of reasons, from religion, personal preference and avoiding addictive behaviours they have observed in their relatives, to health, taste or sheer disinterest. Experimenting with alcohol and drinking to excess as part of the 'rite of passage' into adulthood is in decline. One UK study into drinking culture showed that

16–25-year-olds were most likely to be teetotal.[2] In the US, teetotalism has risen in college-age students from 20 per cent to 28 per cent,[3] and Gen Z are less likely to drink alcohol compared to those aged 35–54.[4] The trend is seen across high-income European countries, as well as in the States, Australia and New Zealand.[5]

What's behind this trend towards sensible consumption and even abstention? It's a complex picture. Younger people are more aware of health and wellbeing than ever before, and well versed in the risks associated with heavy drinking. They are now acutely aware, in a way that generations before them did not have to be, that any substance-fuelled stupidity could be captured and shared online. In 2019, research carried out by Google showed that 41 per cent of Gen Z associated alcohol with 'vulnerability' and 'anxiety',[6] while 60 per cent of UK Gen Z associated drinking with a loss of control.[7] Nearly half reported that their online image was always at the back of their mind.[8] To a large extent, being drunk is simply not seen as cool, and being sober is becoming more socially acceptable. At the same time, the widespread availability of alcohol alternatives, married with the high cost, further drives young people to avoid consuming it. As what 'youth' looks like shapeshifts, so too will the stereotypes of what it looks like for a young person to grieve. The point remains that to support young people, we need to see beyond the ways in which we expect or accept grief to manifest, and instead understand the nuanced ways it shows up in each individual young griever.

*

Olu stood out at the meet-up, because we only ever had a few young men attend each one. He was tall and dressed in the smart-casual attire now so popular with City bankers. This made sense; Olu worked as an analyst at a bank. He'd arrived late and looking lost. When he approached, he leaned in and said quietly, 'Excuse me … is this the grief thing?' This was often the sheepish question asked by uncertain young people trying to find the meet-up in among all the other pub patrons. He shook my hand and looked immediately embarrassed. 'Sorry, that was a bit formal, wasn't it?' I told him not to worry. It was OK to feel awkward if it was his first time.

Olu was 26 and had come to the meet-up, like many of our male members, at the insistence of his girlfriend. His father had died suddenly just a few weeks shy of Olu's eighteenth birthday. Olu was raised in Peckham, where he still lived, by his Nigerian father and Nigerian-British mother. His mother was a nurse. His father had moved to England to complete his medical degree. The couple met while working at the same hospital when Olu's father was a junior doctor. 'I always found it so cheesy, but Mum always said it was love at first sight, his first day on the ward. He had this presence. She felt comfortable around him. I guess at the time there weren't so many Black or mixed-race people working where she worked, and her parents were Nigerian, so she felt he understood a side to her that other people didn't get.'

Olu described his childhood as simple, but warm and happy, where family was prioritised and education highly valued. 'We weren't the most outwardly affectionate family. Dad didn't say "I love you" a lot but it was there in his actions. He'd sit patiently with me, helping me with my homework. He always taught us education was important. It changed his life, and he wanted it to change ours, too.' Olu's father was playful and would indulge his children in their favourite games. 'He'd do our bath-times, too, which wasn't as common in our community for dads. Being a doctor, I think, made him more involved in how we were brought up. He had a gentle way of speaking, which made me feel calm and safe.' To his father, family was everything, and he would revisit Nigeria to see his relatives once a year. 'I'd been out a couple of times with him and was just getting to know that side of things.' Just as Mia spoke of her changing relationship with her mother, Olu felt like he was at an age where he was redefining his relationship with his father as he explored his own identity and what kind of man he wanted to be. 'It made it a really strange time for him to pass.'

Olu was in his final year of school. With his father's encouragement, he had applied to Oxford University to read economics. His father had gone with him on the train to the interview. To his and his father's delight, he was given a conditional offer. Though Olu was studious, and knew he needed to be in order to meet the offer, he was also starting to explore with his friends. 'Some of them were turning 18. They'd started drinking quite a bit; there were always parties on the weekend or hanging out at the park or something. I remember lots of nights wandering down Rye Lane. We knew which shops wouldn't ask for ID. You know, we did a lot of dumb stuff. I remember really clearly the sense of freedom it gave me, despite there being a culture clash. It seemed so normal for me to go out and party with friends, but Dad was more conservative, more religious, and he'd raised me going to church, too. He'd want me there on Sunday mornings, but sometimes I'd have come home late and be hungover. Mum did the mum thing of covering for me. I think, growing up here, she understood it a bit more.'

Olu was excited about the future and moving away from London. But in late May, in the midst of studying for his A levels, he got the call. 'It was Saturday and it was hot. I'd taken the day off revision; I was playing football in the park with my mate. We were messing around, running around like when you score goals – shirts over our heads and stuff. My phone was in my bag, so I didn't see the calls until I went to check. I can still feel the sweat on me, you know, when I picked up my phone.' When he called his mother back, he could hear the sobbing before she spoke. 'It's like, I knew in that moment. I knew and I didn't know. I remember thinking, *I don't want to hear this, whatever it is. I can just be playing football with my friend.* And I could hear beeps in the background, and I knew she was in hospital.' His father had collapsed and had been taken to the hospital where he worked. Olu saw some of his colleagues on the way in. By the time he arrived, his father had already died.

Olu's father had suffered a pulmonary embolism. He died with Olu's mother and siblings by his side at the hospital. Olu still felt guilty for not having been there. 'I remember getting there. Mum was holding Dad's hand and had my little brother and sister clinging onto her. I felt this immediate guilt that, you know, I wasn't there with my family, I wasn't part of that picture. Maybe I'd already felt a bit like I'd taken the day off. I was supposed to be at home studying, but I wasn't. My dad was all about protecting his family and I hadn't done it.' Olu knelt by his father's bedside and took his hand – something he'd rarely done when his father was alive. He noticed the coolness of his father's skin, and he tried to say goodbye. As he left, he couldn't fathom that it would be the last time he'd see his father. 'I kept thinking that when we got home, we'd open the door and he'd be there. I literally just couldn't understand that he wouldn't.'

That afternoon, people began showing up to pay their respects and to bring food to the family. 'It was surreal. This house – I had left in the morning and Dad was alive. When we got home it was so silent and strange, like he would come around the corner from the living room and it would be like it was literally just a nightmare. Then people started turning up, mostly from Mum and Dad's church, but also other people from the community.' Olu found the experience surreal, as if everyone would suddenly disappear from the space and he would wake up to normality. It was from that day he also began to feel the pressure to fill his father's shoes. 'In Nigerian culture, it's very much people saying, *Be strong for your mum*, or aunties saying, *You're the man of the house now*. I already felt that pressure for myself, but it was a lot to be reminded of it. I look back and it's like, I was 17. I was still so young. It's strange for someone to say that to you when you're just a child yourself.' I asked if Olu felt he'd been forced into adulthood. 'Oh, 100 per cent. Big time. My childhood was done,' he said.

'My sister found the community thing strange. She's a bit more introverted than me, probably more similar to Dad. We haven't talked about it a lot, but one time, she told me, she remembers just wanting it to be us that day, you know. Like them all being there disturbed this space where we could have still felt connected to Dad, because he had just been there. She wanted to lock herself in her room and not be dealing with random aunties, you know? It was people who hadn't necessarily been around much for him when he was alive. Like people quite distant from my dad, and I think she felt like, *Why are you showing up now, and telling us to be strong?*'

There were further cultural differences when it came to planning Olu's father's funeral. 'My family in Nigeria thought Dad should be buried over there. He went back every year, but he'd lived here since he was a young man – 30 years or something. They almost had this entitlement. And this assumption, I think, that because we live in London and Dad was a doctor, we were cashed up. There's a lot of money and family politics in African funerals; I think I was expected to deal with some of it because I was the "man of the house", but Mum stepped in to protect me from those conversations. I remember her being exhausted by it. She couldn't understand how they had no empathy for what we, his actual close family, were going through, and how hard it would be for us to make those arrangements, to take him out there. We wouldn't have been able to visit his grave like we do now. I'm glad that she fought for that.'

In the end, the family settled on a celebration service prior to the funeral service. The two occasions were a blend of British and Nigerian cultures that Olu says beautifully reflected his father's life. 'He would have been happy that it was representative of those two cultures, and particularly that it was still culturally very Nigerian. The celebration service is exactly that – a celebration. You go to show your appreciation for their life; you show your love, your thanks. It's quite joyful. It was a very loud, energetic service at the Pentecostal church near us. There was lots of singing. It was, yeah, very loud; it was good.'

The service brought back childhood memories for Olu of going to church with his family. 'It was nice because Dad was normally so calm and quite gentle and, yeah, not emotional. But at church he would get into it, almost like it was a release. Obviously, he had his faith, but it also seemed like this moment where maybe some of that responsibility – of him taking his job so seriously, and his family, and all that – came off his shoulders. He was very thankful for what he had, for the life he had built.

Watching people who'd come from all over – flown over – singing and dancing, that was really nice. It was a nice way to remember him, and I almost felt as if he could be there, and if he'd been there, he would've enjoyed it.'

After finishing his A levels, Olu felt torn. He knew the importance his father placed on education, but he also wanted to stay with his family and help look after them. He decided to defer his place at Oxford for a year, and took up a job working for a friend's father's local business. 'That whole first year I felt numb. I don't remember much of it, if I'm honest.' I told Olu this was something I'd heard was very common for those experiencing a sudden death. 'That's good to know.' Olu entered a period of sobriety. He stopped going out as much with his friends and rarely drank when he did. 'I felt like I couldn't. Dad would have been wanting me to get my head down. I felt this extra responsibility. I didn't want Mum to worry and I wanted my siblings to have some stability. I would go to church with Mum, and I felt closer to Dad if I didn't drink much.' Olu stayed close to his father by stepping into his shoes, helping his mother organise a trip to visit his family in Nigeria so a celebration could be held there for his father. 'Normally it would have been Dad booking the flights, so I helped Mum figure out things like that – things he'd normally have done.'

When Olu went to university the next year, he noticed how much more serious he felt in comparison to other undergraduates. 'I didn't get drunk. I studied. I'd drink maybe one or two drinks on a night out, but I never went mad like other people did. I always went to supervisions, I never missed deadlines. I wasn't into, you know, chasing girls like some of my friends. I felt like I had this duty that my friends didn't have and, to be honest, weren't going to understand.' He graduated with first-class honours. The graduation ceremony was a bittersweet day. 'The night before I remember almost feeling quite bad. It's this thing that I should be so happy about, but all I could think of was Dad and like, why wasn't he here? I couldn't believe he wasn't here to see it. Of my parents, Dad cared more about this stuff. Obviously, Mum was so proud of me and happy and all that, but it was Dad who really cared about education. So that was a strange day. I enjoyed it in the end, but the night before I struggled to find the meaning if he wasn't there to see it.'

Once Olu started working for the bank, he could afford to move out of home. He chose to rent in Peckham, to keep close to his family. He had a reputation at work for being one of the more serious young graduates, in a culture that was often alcohol-focused. 'I did get teased a bit. I just wanted to keep my head down. The other grads, they were living it up more, but I had this sense that I was trying to get to a place of not feeling like everything could be taken away from me in a minute. I struggled with the pressure of it. Now, you'd probably say I was coping with anxiety, but I needed to feel like everything was controlled. It's only recently in the last year or two that that's eased up.' Olu attributes some of that change to his girlfriend, whom he spoke about with warmth and lightness. 'She's so much like Mum, like the life and soul. They get on really well; they try to bring out the fun side in me more. She helps me relax and remember that beyond responsibility, family is also about laughing and sometimes being silly and all that. She was the first person I really spoke to about my dad and how it felt. I spent so much time worrying about Mum and my siblings, I wasn't in touch with the effect it had on me.'

Olu spoke about how being able to talk openly about the thoughts and feelings he'd experienced brought him some comfort. 'I'd never talk to my friends about it now. I don't talk about it a lot. But I do think about Dad all the time. What would he say? What would he want me to do? What would he think of me? Would he be proud? I think he'd be proud. I think, being a guy, Dad wasn't that emotional, so I wasn't used to talking about my feelings. I've been trying to self-educate a bit more now. I've read a few things about grief and your mental health and staying on top of it. My girlfriend helps a lot; she tries to get me to talk about it. The anniversary's coming up soon, so we're planning another trip to Nigeria to see some family. On the one hand, it's been so heavy. It's been a lot of responsibility. On the other hand, I like feeling like I'm Dad's son, and I'm doing the things he'd have done. That's the part that feels lighter – that I'm happy I had him as a dad, and he taught me so much, even if I didn't have him for long.'

Three

First Love

*Falling in love, heartbreak, coming out and
getting laid*

Some months after my mother died, I started dating people
again. I kept her death from all of them. Holding it back felt like
a form of self-preservation; it was too soon and too raw to talk
about with people I couldn't yet trust. If the subject of parents
came up, I'd either still talk about my mother in the present
tense or safely omit her altogether. Holding it back could also
feel like a strange power. In relationships, casual or serious, I'd
often felt like the more available, more invested party. For what
felt like the first time, I knew that these flings meant little to me
beyond the physical or circumstantial, even if they were also
healing or pleasantly distracting. In return, I discovered that
some people were hooked on me the way I'd been hooked on
distant and unavailable partners in the past. Suddenly, I was
being described as 'cagey', 'enigmatic', even 'surprising'. It was

a strange experience, finding myself on the other side of emotional unavailability. But sex was not just some superficial distraction: it felt like a significant counterbalance to grief. Both experiences were so physical, had the potential to be so over-whelming, that physical intimacy allowed me to return to the world, to feel anchored to life, to vitality, to my senses, when I so often felt like I was without time, structure or reality.

It was only when I returned to Melbourne, where I had lived and worked for two years before my mother died, that I met someone who made it easy for me to talk about her death. I wasn't still supposed to be there the day I met Lewis. I'd gone back for a month over January to catch the summer and skip the European winter. I couldn't face the prolonged cold and dark that was so viscerally associated with my last months in Berlin, and the last months of my mother's life. Arriving in the heat was a relief. Melbourne felt much more like home than where I'd grown up and I'd missed it desperately. My old friends welcomed me back with open arms and empathy, in full knowl-edge of what I'd been through. One of my closest friends there, Jo, had lost her father to cancer after four years of illness, shortly before my mother died. Jo and I would drive to the beach in her father's old car, which she loved, listening to the local radio playing little-known lo-fi Melbourne bands. We'd sunbathe and read, and talk about grief and boys and girls and where we wanted to go out later. One evening, she and some others convinced me to stay in Melbourne a few weeks longer. The next weekend, I met Lewis at a friend's birthday party.

I'd cycled to the pub a little hungover from the night before. Standing up tall from my pedals, I built up speed along the Upfield Bike Path – the long cycle route that hugs the trainline north through the suburb of Brunswick – and as I snaked past the tracks and the gum trees, I felt a burst of joy at the freedom of it. In my baggy jeans and sandals, the warm air skating the skin of my bare arms, I felt something akin to bliss. It had an edge to it – an intensity I knew hadn't been there before, sharpened in contrast to the pain I had experienced since my mother's diagnosis and death. When Lewis walked into the pub a few hours later, it was hard to believe: that I could already feel this content, and then be meeting this ridiculously good-looking Australian on top. He was so genuinely attractive, I struggled to speak to him at all. It was he who struck up a conversation. Throughout the course of the night, I mentioned easily and naturally that my mother had died eight months ago. He didn't try to gloss over it. He just listened and tried to empathise. Long after my other friends had left, he gave me a lift home at golden hour, my bike folded awkwardly into the back of his station wagon. I remember thinking that nothing as romantic had happened to me for years, laughing with this boy who was so funny and caring and interested, as the light crept over the dashboard and lit up the terraced houses along the streets of Brunswick. When I walked through the door of the flat where I was staying, my friends looked at me expectantly. I fake-swooned and declared, 'I think I'm in love!'

But I wasn't 'in love'. I fell for Lewis very differently to how I'd fallen for my previous boyfriend. Although I felt myself connect to him immediately, I could only let it happen incrementally, ceding small ground day by day. I sensed the caution. I was hyper-aware of how he treated me, hyper-aware of my own emotional capacity. Where I had been overly giving and caring in past relationships, I was now reticent and more withholding. I was unwilling to give emotionally if I felt I wouldn't get it back. Lewis never pushed me for more, though. He allowed me to be myself and was enamoured with every small revelation of my personality, coaxing out sides to me that I'd never thought were valuable. My confidence grew. He supported me in building myself back up when I had shut so much of myself down.

Falling in love for the first time without my mother to report it to was strange. I would have told her almost everything, and I'd find myself imagining what she would have said to me and how pleased she would have been that I'd found someone who treated me with such care. She would have found Lewis so funny, and I could picture them ganging up on me, teasing me mercilessly, if they'd ever met. Sometimes in the morning, in the soft hour before the world starts to turn, I would look at Lewis in bed through sleep-thin eyes and think that, although my mother's love could never be replaced, his was a kind of kindred care. I was accepted and loved for who I was. Although I knew it as a fact, I still couldn't believe that he would never meet her. That these two people whose love felt so profound would never set eyes upon each other or speak a word in exchange.

Lewis and I broke up eventually (long distance; pandemic), but he remains one of the people I feel most comfortable talking to about my grief. He will still sit and listen on FaceTime, drinking his morning coffee as I bawl my eyes out if grief is keeping me up past midnight in London. He will still build me up when the grief-fear makes me doubt myself and my abilities in other aspects of my life. He held me in that most fragile time, and that is an intimacy that will never truly fade.

Intimacy, physical or emotional, is a complex thing for any griever. To expose yourself, as intimacy demands, when you already feel vulnerable can be terrifying. For quarter-life grievers in particular, intimacy and relationships are aspects of young-adult life that can already be sources of insecurity. How grief layers over that terrain is unique for every individual. At meet-ups, I would hear stories of how physical intimacy could be, as it was for me, a relief. Sex was so immersive that it washed away the numbness of grief, the physicality of it pinning you to the present moment when the rest of your life felt adrift. Even with a stranger and in the absence of sentiment, the erotic could be a salve. Although sexual promiscuity is another negative limb of the 'hot mess young person' stereotype (often particularly for women), it was possible for many of the young grievers I spoke with to engage in it without feeling emotionally vulnerable. It could instead offer respite from difficult emotions. For others, it was not so straightforward.

Kate Moyle, a sexual and relationship psychotherapist who hosts the *Sexual Wellness Sessions* podcast, says that there are an infinite number of ways loss can affect someone's sexual and emotional intimacy. 'A lot of issues around sex are to do with control. It comes up with everyone I speak to. So there are different ways grief can affect this need for control. Sex can be terrifying if you are already in this "out-of-control" space of grief. On the other hand, some people end up pushing the "fuck it" button and think, *Well, if* that *can happen at any time, I want to feel, I want to explore, I want to play and feel alive*, and that's something sex can offer.'

If sex could offer succour, relationships were typically more difficult to navigate. For those I spoke to, in new romances, deciding when to reveal their grief and not knowing how the other person would respond was always a live question. In long-term relationships, grief could raise existing fault lines or show that the partner in question wasn't emotionally supportive, spelling the end. Meeting someone's family for the first time could be a very present, very visual reminder that their partner's 'unit' was complete (or 'normal') and theirs was not. Coming to terms with their sexuality, when they had no opportunity to tell the bereaved, was complicated. Some young grievers reported seeking out new relationships in a bid to fill the gap, sometimes leading to unhealthy relationships where the new partner took advantage of their vulnerability. 'For some, their natural instinct may be to shut down and turn away from intimacy and connection,' Moyle states, 'whereas for others, there may be this need to "cling on" and to replace the connection.' When you are young and your model for connections and bonds is still evolving, grief can have a lasting impact on how you love and lose again.

*

Immy came to one of the first meet-ups I ever ran. She was tall, blonde and stylish. I remember admiring her well-manicured nails as she sipped her wine. She looked traditionally feminine and attractive. After her mother's death, she found herself enjoying sexual promiscuity, but she was troubled by realising she was attracted to women as well as men. Elegant presentation was something she told me she had picked up from her mother, who died when Immy was 25. 'She never left the house without lipstick. Even in hospital, she put make-up on every day. I hated the idea that cancer was taking away this thing she prided herself on.' The cancer had been aggressive and swift: Immy's mother died within six months of diagnosis.

After her death, Immy kept her mother's old make-up case and would use her mother's favourite lipstick when going out.

'I had never worn those shades before, but I was almost surprised how much it suited me. That sounds stupid because of course I had her colouring. It was comforting and almost felt like a ritual that kept her close and present.' One Saturday night, a couple of months after her mother's death, Immy went out to a bar with friends. There, she bumped into a boy she had known briefly at university. 'I remember while we were saying hi, I caught this look he gave me and I realised: *Oh, I can just have that. I can go home with him. He's clearly interested*. It was strange because I'd been so focused on my grief that it came as a surprise that I could still be attractive to people on the outside. I ended up ignoring him all evening and then picking him up as I was leaving. I thought, *God, is that what it's like to be a guy? Is it this easy?*'

The sex allowed Immy to feel present for the first time since her mother's death. 'It was this moment of: *I'm here again. I'm in my body for the first time in months*. The grief slipped away. I could almost feel it physically creeping back the next morning. I remember turning Radio 4 on and it hit me, because I'd struggled to listen to it since Mum died. She always put it on while making breakfast. But it almost felt manageable, because I'd had this break the night before. It was nice to realise that I didn't have to feel the grief constantly.' Immy started to go on dates with men from dating apps, or those she met through friends. She didn't want a relationship, but she did want sex. 'I don't want to make out that it was wild or unsafe, or that anyone would do. I still had to like them and enjoy talking to them. I was always clear I didn't want intimacy. I wanted it to be fast or overwhelming, always very physical, sometimes rough. Anything that would give me immersion, so that all I could focus on was my body and my brain would turn off. And it was *fun*, because I couldn't give a fuck if one day a guy stopped texting me back, because there was always another one. That was very different – truly not caring.' She never told the men she dated about her mother and it acted as a 'very clear boundary' for her. 'I feel like I was raised, like a lot of girls, to put guys and their feelings first. For once, I was putting myself first.'

While Immy experienced liberation and distraction with men, connecting to her physicality came with an added surprise. She realised she was also attracted to women. Yet where sex with men came easily, with women her feelings were entirely different. She could never stop thinking about what her mother would make of it. 'I remember for me growing up, I never thought being gay was bad or wrong. People came out at school, and it wasn't cool to be homophobic towards them. But Mum was kind of homophobic. Not outwardly so; she wouldn't have called anyone the F-word. She'd had gay friends at work, but she was of the generation who wanted gay people to not exist publicly. She'd squirm if there was a gay kiss on TV, or she'd make comments about how manly lesbians looked. She was very uncomfortable with it.'

Her mother had always assumed Immy and her sister were straight, without realising how her remarks about gay people would discourage them from exploring their sexual identities. 'I think because I did like boys, and Mum's favourite thing was to be nosy about boys me and my sister fancied, there was never any question. I never questioned it myself. I thought about kissing girls sometimes, and I did when I was drunk as a teenager and at uni, but I just brushed it off as curiosity or playing up to the male lesbian porn fantasy. Although, I had always been adamant about never doing it for male attention. Looking back, those kisses were all genuine.'

The moment Immy realised she wasn't straight came when she reunited with an old colleague who she had worked with before her mother's death. 'I worked at this creative agency in London where a lot of the staff were young, cool twenty-somethings. Everyone was so much cooler than me. I felt like an impostor, wearing camel coats like a suburban mum. There was one girl, Eimear, who was very androgynous, or what I've now learnt you would call "soft butch". She had short, dark hair and dressed quite boyish. Obviously, I'm the opposite. Immediately, I took a shine to her. She was Irish and very funny and sort of the office joker. I so desperately wanted her to think I was cool and funny, and I distinctly remember hoping that she would "look past" my appearance.' Immy often found herself teasing Eimear, or discussing *RuPaul's Drag Race* with her, to show she was aware of queer culture. She'd sometimes bump into Eimear at the same Tube stop in the morning. Immy felt a thrill at walking the five minutes to the office with her, even though she had no idea why. Immy left the company just before her mother died but had arranged to see her old colleagues some months after her mother's death. Eimear would be there.

'I remember thinking about what it would be like to see everyone again. There was a grotty nightclub people from work would go to after the pub sometimes. I'd never been – I hated hanging out with colleagues after work that late. But I remember thinking, *Maybe we'll all end up at the nightclub*. And then I thought, *Maybe we'll all be drunk*. And then I thought, *Maybe Eimear and I will make out when we're drunk*. And as *soon* as I thought that, I thought, *Oh fuck*. This whole time, I'd thought I'd just been trying to be Eimear's friend. But it wasn't that – it was that I *fancied* her! The reason I teased her was because I was flirting with her. The reason I wanted her to "look past" my appearance was because I wanted her not to think I was straight. Because I wasn't.'

So, what happened with Eimear? I was hoping for a happy, romantic ending. 'Turns out she had a girlfriend,' said Immy. 'She'd never talked about her at work, but they were planning on moving in together. It sucked. I like to think the night I saw her, there was chemistry. There were ways our eyes would catch when we spoke that [made me think], *Yeah, maybe if she was single, it would have happened.*' Though Immy felt happy to have worked out what she felt for Eimear, the wider implication that her sexual identity was different to what she'd assumed frightened her. How could she not have known this important thing about herself? Why was she only just discovering it in the turmoil of grief? The timing felt too symbolic to ignore.

'I didn't know how to feel about it. I was worried about what my mum would have thought. I worried it would have disgusted her. I also knew I felt angry at her for the part she played in suppressing that part of myself, but it felt awful to feel angry at someone I loved so much and who I missed so much. We were so close and the idea of if I'd come out to her, and I'd been met with ignorance or not fully accepted, that breaks my heart.' To add to the difficulty, Immy's family dynamic had shifted since her mother's death. Her sister, now an investment banker who Immy felt had always been seen as the 'successful' child, was trying to take on the same role that her mother had occupied. At the same time, her father began seeing a new woman within a year of Immy's mother's death. If Immy had already found it hard to be herself with her mother, the family member she was closest to, she certainly didn't feel that she could 'show up' with her queerness to her grieving family.

At the same time, Immy found that her new realisation impacted on her sense of identity. 'I don't want to conflate gender and sexuality because obviously you can look very feminine, like my sister, and be a lesbian, or you can look like Eimear and be straight. But I'd always found the effort you had to put into looking "female", which seemed so easy and enjoyable for my mum and my sister, was a chore. Suddenly I wanted to cut my hair short and get a septum piercing and wear shirts. On the other hand, I knew how I looked worked for me in terms of sleeping with guys. And changing my appearance was like changing the version of me that my mum knew.' The confusion was not unique to Immy; the biphobia she feared facing in the queer community made it equally difficult to accept her sexual identity. 'I didn't have *loads* of gay friends at uni. I always remembered how straight girls who went to gay bars were considered "tourists" or [to be] ruining it for gay men. Or the stereotype that bisexual girls were basically straight girls who were just "using" lesbians or were not serious or were not truly queer. There's a question of validity. I did find myself thinking, *Am I just a straight girl who's gone mad with grief and suddenly thinks she's into girls?* I have found it very difficult trying to date any girls for fear of rejection.' For Immy, the isolating effects of grief were pervasive: she felt cut off from a community she wished to be a part of, insulated herself from the men she saw, and felt adrift from her mother and family as her own sense of self grew.

Immy found support through therapy and a friend who had come out as bisexual some years before. 'My friend was really a help in understanding that some of these questions about validity are questions most bisexual people struggle with. She's also struggled with her appearance in terms of wanting to signal she's queer but still being quite feminine. The difference was that her mum is very supportive and she obviously had the chance to talk about it.' In therapy, Immy was helped in trying to have the conversation with her mother she never had. 'Even though I was never fully able to access my mum's "voice", I was able to realise that she loved me unconditionally. The fact that I'm attracted to women wouldn't have stopped her from loving me, whether she would have been open to learning more about queerness or not.' Immy was able to tell her sister but didn't feel ready to be fully open with her father. 'Although the other day he did call me and said something about when I find my "Mr (or Mrs!) Right", which was the first time in 28 years that either of my parents have said something that signals it's OK to be gay. It's been difficult with him seeing other people, but one good influence they have had is maybe a slightly more liberal outlook. I know that he loves me, and I know that my mum loved me, and I guess that's the most important thing. The rest is a work in progress.'

*

As Immy's experience shows, quarter-life grief asks us to become independent from someone we depended on before we are ready. While that independence can become positive self-sufficiency, it can also easily tip into 'hyper-independence', a common trauma coping mechanism that keeps us isolated from new attachments. This was a theme that came up when I spoke to Kenny Ethan Jones about the death of his parents, who died within seven months of one another in 2015 and 2016, when Kenny was 21 and 22. Kenny is an activist, entrepreneur and former model who made history as the first trans man to front a period campaign. He has walked at London Fashion Week, and his work has been featured in *Vogue, them,* the *Daily Mail* and more. When we speak, he is confident, personable and handsome. As he talks, his face lights up with a wide, knowing smile, exuding drive and focus. While Kenny always knew he was a 'name-in-lights' kind of person, he found it was his relationships that were most affected after the deaths of his parents.

'I'd say my story starts with me being 18,' he says. 'I'd just started testosterone and was about to get top surgery.' (Top surgery removes breast tissue and 'masculinises' the chest. It is part of the medical transition to being male.) 'Mum was always my main parent. Dad lived 10 minutes away and had 11 other kids, so he didn't have the same time to get to know us all fully. He wasn't as accepting of my transition when I was younger, but he was just coming to a point of acceptance. He'd stopped using my old name. He'd call me K or Kenny, and use he/him pronouns.' Kenny describes his mother as his best friend. 'She was such a big pillar in my support system. She'd be the one chasing up my transition appointments or doing my injections. She was so protective, she'd literally fight for me.' At the same time, her doctors had warned Kenny that his mother might not live for much longer. She was 53 and had suffered from alcoholism and cancer when Kenny was still in secondary school. 'They told me she wouldn't live past 60.'

When Kenny was 20, he moved to Prague to take up an exciting new job. 'My relationship with Mum was still good, although I didn't hug her as much anymore 'cause, like, I'm a man now, I don't wanna do that,' he says, grinning. Between the intensity of his new job and navigating a new city, Kenny had little time to speak to his mother directly over the phone. Gradually, though, through voice notes she sent him, he started to sense that she wasn't in good health. Despite asking his friends at home to check in on her, Kenny felt compelled to come home. 'There was this day – I woke up in the morning and, I don't know why, but something was telling me to go. My body was saying, *Move – you need to go home now*. I've never felt such a strong instinct. I couldn't physically ignore it. I was broke at this point so I had to ask a friend to pay for my ticket home. He asked me if I was sure. I said, "I've never been so sure of something in my life. I'm getting on a plane tonight."'

Kenny quit his job and travelled back to London. His mother cried when she saw him. Kenny finally saw the full extent of his mother's ill health: she was breathing heavily, drinking at night, and couldn't walk through the hallway without clinging onto the walls and doors for support. Kenny knew he needed her to attend a hospital, but she hated them. Together with his sister (his mother's first child, with a different father), Kenny got his mother to go. Despite the difficulty of the time, he smiles when remembering his mum's reaction. 'Her sense of humour is very "cussy". She's Liverpudlian so that says it all. At the hospital, they're trying to ask her who the Queen is, what year it is, and she's brushing it off like, *Fuck off, I'm not listening to this bollocks*.' Kenny managed to convince his mother to stay and hear the doctors' prognosis. Overnight, his mother was placed in an induced coma and moved to intensive care. On seeing her hooked up to various tubes and medical equipment, his sister collapsed to the floor. 'She was in frantic tears and I tried to hold it together. When I looked at Mum, though, I could see she's got her legs in these things they use to keep her muscles going, and tubes down her throat to help her breathe, and her kidneys are failing so she's attached to a kidney machine, and there's a bag collecting shit at the end of the bed. I was in complete shock. How had her body completely shut down like this, so quickly? And I knew that was it. I wasn't going to get a chance to speak to her again. I just started crying. I didn't know what else to do in that moment.'

After four weeks in intensive care, the decision was made to turn off Kenny's mother's life support. He and his sister sat by her side as her body shut down. 'She'd lost a lot of siblings and her parents, so we told her she was going to be with them. We said, "We know it's hard for you to leave us, but we're grateful for the time we had, and it's your time now. And then she just went."' Standing outside the hospital at nine o'clock in the morning, Kenny watched commuters rushing to work, people absorbed in their phones, the city heaving into life. 'I felt absolutely nothing. I felt this encompassing feeling of just black. It felt like I was in a movie. Everyone was going about their day-to-day and my life had completely changed. I don't remember how I got home from the hospital. I just remember being at home and thinking, *Well, what do I do now?* I had no idea how to move forward.'

In the following months, Kenny locked himself away in his mother's house. 'I literally just drank. I'd always linked alcohol to fun and good times. I just wanted something lighter than what I was experiencing.' His friends would try to check on him, but he told them to leave him alone. 'It got to a point where I'd write a note on my front door saying, *If you knock on my door, I'll knock you out.* I was so angry. I felt like something had been stolen from me.' He struggled to pay the rent on his mother's house, with no sympathy from his landlord. 'It was council-owned and the first thing they try to do is get you to move, because you're one person taking up a two-bed.' Kenny found himself having to do all the things that had previously been done for him: paying bills, cooking, taking care of his mother's dogs. The arrival of these new responsibilities was abrupt, and it took time for him to find his feet.

Just as Kenny felt he'd moved past the initial shock of his mother's death, his father fell ill. 'He'd never been sick a day in his life. I'd never seen that man even have a cold. He was a very traditional Caribbean man – home remedies, home-cooked food, all that sort of stuff.' His father had cancer. He'd hidden his diagnosis from his son in order to protect him in the imme- diate aftermath of his mother's death. Although he had the option of chemotherapy, he ultimately decided to make the most of the time he had left. Kenny supported his decision and encouraged him to go back to Jamaica to spend time with his family, who still lived there.

Unlike with his mother, Kenny had time to express his love for his father. 'It was sad because it was the first time we had a friendship. It was the first time he'd really seen me and gotten to grips with my personality and how strong I am. I had a motor- bike at the time, and he loved motorbikes. He told me about the time he crashed his bike in Jamaica when he was younger. Everyone said it was karma because he was cheating on his girl- friend and the other girl was on the back.' He laughs as he recalls the story. 'He was giving me life lessons, saying, "Don't do that!" We'd never talked about hobbies or been on that level. He'd always seen me as the odd kid. The others had more "normal" lives. I was the troublesome one. It was heart- breaking to have reached this point of friendship when he was dying. He told me he should have been more supportive when I told him I was trans. He said, "I should have respected you and your decisions, but you was young and I didn't really know what to think. In Jamaica, this just doesn't happen."'

Kenny and his siblings arranged his father's Nine Nights, the traditional Caribbean funerary tradition, and his funeral. 'He didn't have a funeral plan, but my siblings wanted it to be the traditional elaborate, expensive thing, and we had a big family, so we had to cater to that. That was tense because I was 21, I didn't have much money, and I wanted to spend what I had on looking after myself, and doing the things other twenty-somethings are doing.' Once his father's funeral had passed, Kenny realised the significance of having lost both his parents. 'There are some things I'll just never know. Only your parents know these things. I hadn't asked a lot of questions about my childhood because at 20, 21, that wasn't interesting to me – the future was. When my dad died, I realised, *Wow, I'm losing my history. I'm losing the opportunity for my parents to meet my kids if I ever have them. They're never going to meet the person I love and marry.* It felt all-encompassing.'

His parents' deaths made Kenny particularly uncomfortable at the idea of depending on anyone else. He found he was only able to love with caution, fearing the next loss that might happen. 'Where grief has been the biggest burden is in my relationships,' he says. 'My ability to love and to connect with people has definitely suffered.' He felt a loss of identity that made it difficult for him to open up to others. 'Everyone felt so sorry for me, and I'd never wanted to be that person. Even with all the other obstacles I'd had in my life – being trans, being Black – I've never, ever wanted someone to feel sorry for me. The idea that I was this strong, ambitious man, and now I'm just a kid who lost his parents, that was hard because it made me feel vulnerable. In response, there was lots of destructive behaviour, lots of drinking, lots of disconnecting myself from people.'

Kenny entered various relationships but found it hard to connect on a deep level. 'Some of my relationships were lovely and I cared about them deeply, and parts of me loved them, but I knew they were never going to be my person. Part of it was that I'd had to learn so much to look after myself after Mum died, and I just never wanted to get back into that situation where someone is everything to me and I lose them.' Kenny's insistence on being completely self-sufficient has stopped him from having the healthy inter-dependency that intimate relationships require. 'I just don't want people to do things for me because it makes it easier if I do it all for myself, so I don't feel dependent on other people. It's like I've built my own "house" and I don't need anyone in it. I don't need people. I'm fine, I've got this. I think that comes from Mum having been such a big pillar in my support system. When she died, I had to figure all that out on my own. I might have been 21, but you're still a child, let's be honest. I suddenly realised how much she'd done for me, like washing up or paying bills – all these silly things you don't notice. Financially, I had to take care of myself, too. I never want to have to go through losing that again, so I don't let people get close.'

Most of the people Kenny dated were not the right fit, but he'd fall into relationships anyway. 'I knew they weren't forever, but in moments, I would get a good vibe and we'd get along, and I'd attach myself to them because it was comfortable. It was always that situation from one person to the next. I wanted to feel less alone, but I was still pushing people away and saying I don't need anyone.' Many of Kenny's exes connected the dots of his bad behaviour with his grief, even when he didn't tell them explicitly what was going on. 'It felt like they'd seen me as special and wanted to take care of me. They understood grief was part of the reason why we [weren't] progressing in our relationships, 'cause there'd be moments where I'd completely shut down or be rude. They'd tell me, "This is because of your parents," and they'd acknowledge that I was angry. But it was the reason quite a few of my exes left me. It was a recurring thing in my relationships.'

On top of wanting to be self-sufficient, Kenny felt he couldn't open up to his partners about his grief because they wouldn't understand. 'When I landed the period campaign in 2018, I knew I was making history. I was the first trans man to feature and that's such a big achievement. There's not many people that get to say, "I made history." The one person I wanted to share that with was my mum. I remember wanting to call her and it felt like, at that moment, I could somehow. I went to grab my phone, and then it just made me sad and I got teary-eyed. My girlfriend at the time asked me if I was OK, but I didn't know how to explain what I'd experienced. She hadn't gone through loss so I didn't think she would get it. I just kept it to myself.'

Like Immy, Kenny found that his grief also affected his relationships as he made new discoveries about his sexuality. Soon after his father died, he found himself flying on a whim to Houston, to meet a man he had talked to over Instagram. 'I really played myself,' he laughed. 'I'd convinced myself I was going because this was a good new business contact. It didn't take long when I got there to realise it was something else.' Kenny had never found himself attracted to men before. While he had a good time in Houston, the realisation brought his gender identity back into doubt. 'At the time, I'd considered myself to be straight. I'd just transitioned to being a man, I liked women, but now I'm attracted to a man? I worried it invalidated my masculinity a bit. Eventually, I understood that obviously gender and sexuality are completely separate things. It didn't make me less of a man to be sexually into men. Now I'd describe myself as pansexual and I'm ambivalent about monogamy. But at the time, it would have been good to talk to my mum about it. She would have been fine with it; she'd have been like, *Send me all his pics!* She'd have wanted to know everything.'

In relationships with men, Kenny felt particularly confronted by the loss of his father. 'I started to attach myself to men more sexually. I'm not sure about the psychology of it, but I think there's something in there about losing your father and losing that bond and connection with your father, and wanting more attention and connection with men. I missed that male relationship in my life. I was processing that while I was seeing guys.' Again, although some of the men he dated saw the connection, Kenny wasn't willing to explore it openly with them. 'I cheated on one of my ex-boyfriends a couple of times, which is obviously something I'm not proud of. He realised, though, more than I did, that there was a connection there between my dad dying and me hooking up with these people. He wanted to take the time to explore it, but I wasn't there yet. I didn't want to face up to it being something about losing Dad. It's only as you get older and you see the behaviour repeating that it makes you want to understand yourself better, and you ask yourself, *Why am I like this?*'

When we talk, Kenny is dating the bestselling author and presenter Megan Crabbe, who is known for her work in body positivity and mental health awareness. The relationship is one where Kenny feels he has been able to begin to address some of his hyper-independence. His tone changes as he speaks about her and the impact their relationship has had on how he frames emotional intimacy. 'Now I'm in this situation where I'm with someone who just … sets my soul alight. You know? Where this person, it's not just that they're the person for you, but they're good for you and all the dots connect and it's perfect. But I did have this sense of: *I want to love you, and I do love you, but something is holding us back.*'

Megan has made a concerted effort to get the relationship onto 'solid ground'. 'She said to me, "I want you to need me." And I said, "I don't need anybody."' Kenny explained to her how deeply his sense of independence and self-sufficiency were rooted. 'I told her, "Take all the people closest to me: you, my sister, my best friend. I don't *need* any of you. When I lost my mum, I felt I was the only one that could take care of [me]. If I can lose someone that significant in my life and it can happen again, I don't want to go back to that. What happens if I allow you to become my everything and I lose you? Then I'm back to being that kid who lost his mum. I don't want to go there. I can't do that again." It's one of the first things I'll say if we're having a hard time in the relationship. I say, "What happens when you die and I'm here having to deal with it?" It comes out. I'm not thinking about it when I say it; it just rolls off my tongue, so I know that fear runs deep.'

Despite this, Kenny has started to share memories of his mother with Megan. It is one of the healthier ways he has started to process his loss, to break down the barrier of wanting to stay completely independent in relationships. 'There will be random moments [when] I'll just start laughing, and I'll explain to her why. For example, there was a period in time – I don't even know why – that Mum used to fall off the toilet seat. She just wasn't physically capable of sitting on it. We had a wonky toilet seat for years that she refused to fix, so I'd just hear her falling off it sometimes from down the hall. I did it once recently because the toilet seat is broken at the moment and I was just on the floor, pissing myself laughing. Megan asked me why it was so funny, and I told her the story – that Mum used to do this all the time.'

Kenny has found that sharing his memories of his mother and father has allowed Megan to meet them in some way. It allows him to stay connected with them. 'People see grief as something to want to get over. If I say to my friends, "I miss my mum," some of them are like, "Are you not over that?" Obviously, it's like, "Well, you lose your mum and then we'll have this conversation."' Megan hasn't put that pressure on Kenny. 'She's intelligent and intuitive about it, which has had a good impact on our relationship. She always says to me, "I'd love to hear stories about your mum, if you ever want to talk about her or your dad." She'll take the time to understand whatever memory has come up. Sharing my parents with Megan has made us bond more than I have with exes, because she knows more about me through knowing about my parents.'

It is still a work in progress. 'I'm not at the point where I "need" her yet. And by "need", I don't want to define what it means to other people, but to me it means being able to love someone fully. I don't think I'm capable of that yet. "Needing" for me is loving at full capacity and I still don't feel able to. All the things we're doing together, though, with time, are on the road to achieving it.' I can almost feel Kenny's apprehension as he talks. I tell him that being able to be vulnerable and need someone again is, frankly, fucking terrifying. 'Yeah,' he says. 'You get it. It's like letting go of everything and trusting your life with somebody. Opening yourself up to that level of pain again is scary. But when you shut that out of your life, you're shutting out so much good stuff. Trying to stop the pain means stopping all the good stuff coming in. I think over time you learn to accept [that] grief is part of life, but I don't think the fear will ever go away. I think you adjust to it. It doesn't get any less painful.'

*

Kenny's fear is justified. Of course, everyone we love will die eventually. But in a more immediate sense, when you have been bereaved, any new loss of love (whether through death, heart-break or otherwise) will recall an old loss. As Dennis Klass writes in *Continuing Bonds: New Understandings of Grief*, 'One of the most significant reminders of previous loss is a new loss. The fresh grief for a new loss may often be entangled in grief for other losses, and, quite possibly, each recurrence of grief for one loss may set off grieving for other losses. One implication of grief recurrence is that after one's first major loss, one will never be completely free of grieving.'

That means for quarter-life grievers, it isn't just falling in love or beginning new relationships that is hard. It means those dramatic, heart-wrenching break-ups you go through when you're young have an added element of depth, as they bring back the pain and reality of grief, and the inevitability of loss. This was the case for Emily, a talented editor and writer whose mother died from a brain tumour when she was 25. Now in her early thirties, Emily spoke of a recent break-up that forced her to revisit her feelings about her mother's death. 'It was totally out of the blue and completely felled me,' she wrote of the split. 'So much of it was to do with grief – it was another exam-ple of someone I loved vanishing. For many reasons, I'm thankful we broke up, but one of the main things is that it forced me to address losing my mum. I ended up in Florence after the break-up. My mum spent time here when she was 18. I'm not all that sure about religion but have a sense of the spiritual. On my first day here, I lit a candle for her in San Miniato [a small town west of Florence] and thanked her for giving me the courage to come to a new city on my own. It's just another example of the type of small conversation I have with her every day.'

In her twenties, in the aftermath of her mother's death, Emily had prioritised friendships above romance. 'Watching someone die changes the fabric of who you are. It's such a formative, violent thing. It feels so pervasive. The ongoing illness and slow decline of her death 100 per cent changed and shaped who I am.' When it came to romantic relationships, Emily felt her heart had to be 'this kind of flinty, solid thing, because if it wasn't then I would be a weeping pool of tears'. In that state, there was 'no way' she could pursue a relationship. Instead, her friendships deepened. 'I value my friendships now above and beyond everything. Almost to my detriment – sometimes in romantic relationships I have ended things because that person couldn't see why my friendships were so important.' Like with Kenny, the risk of further heartbreak held her back: 'I felt like, *No one can come anywhere near this. The potential for anyone to cause any more damage to my heart is too high a risk.* It meant that, for a significant stretch of time afterwards, I was just like, *No.*'

This was part of the reason the breakdown of her relationship in her early thirties felt so devastating. Having finally trusted someone, they vanished without a trace. Her ex never explained why he left; they had no contact after he did. But, as

Emily describes it, the man himself had little to do with the pain that came after. He was, perhaps appropriately, eclipsed in the new phase of grief his departure triggered, so far as to be entirely absent from the picture Emily paints when she speaks of the split. 'There is a difference between processing something and feeling sad,' she says slowly. 'Prior to the break-up, I had obviously felt sad about my mum for a long time, but I had slightly put a lid on it. The break-up led to that lid just bursting off. There was a kind of second wave of grief that, frankly, was much more to do with my mum than with the person I'd broken up with. The experience of it, having my heart broken, having quite a long stretch of feeling really shit and awful, was almost more formative than the years directly after my mum died. But it was still part of the same thing.'

Emily realised that the depth of her feelings was not to do with her ex. It was to do with all the unresolved feelings that had gone before. 'I honestly feel like a *totally* different person now to the person I was two or three years ago. Of course, some of this might be to do with getting older. But I needed, maybe, the distance from my mum dying to work out how I felt about it. It had almost been … too hot to touch? Then, having this other thing as a catalyst forced me to look at what happened, and that meant I was able to spend time with those feelings and think about it in a more considered way. It proved to be a really brilliant thing. It gave me a huge amount of strength. I feel much more content with who I am and what I think about things and what I value.' In processing her grief through the new loss, Emily gained a 'much stronger, clearer sense of self'. The change to her outlook is intangible. 'Everything just feels clearer. I've come to recognise time is not infinite and it is my responsibility to use it as I want to use it, with the people I want to use it with. I want to spend my time well, and I want to be with good, energising, dynamic, interesting people. It cleared away some of the murk.'

*

When a young griever has already experienced the loss of love, the fear of losing love again will affect any new attachment. For Paula, a successful TV director, this impact was amplified because the person she lost was her first proper boyfriend. She met Justin at secondary school. 'It was pure cliché,' she laughs. 'Like, totally high school. We were 14, 15. It was raining and the boys had just been playing football, and I saw Justin taking his top off, and I thought, *Wow, he's hot*. But he was really shy – he barely said a word to anyone except his mates – so we didn't actually start talking until a bit later. We used to get the bus together and I remember one day getting on and he just handed me one side of his earphones. That was when I started listening to hip-hop music, because of him.'

Nothing happened straight away. Paula and Justin lived near one another and would see each other regularly during the summer holidays. 'We hung out but never as anything more than friends.' When they both went to different schools for sixth form, their friendship finally transformed into something more. 'One summer, when we were both at different schools, we hooked up. We'd probably always fancied each other. By then, we were both 17. It was June. He turned 18 in September and in March, he had the car accident. So we weren't together long, but when you're 18, that doesn't really matter. You've known this person since you were 15 and you hang out all the time. At 18, the last thing you're thinking is that someone is going to die.'

It was a Friday night. Justin hadn't been reachable on his phone all day, but that wasn't unusual. Paula had got home from school and was about to get into the shower. She got a call from Justin's brother. He called her often to see if she could help get him on guest lists for nights out, so she didn't find it strange for him to be calling. It was only when she heard his voice that she realised something was wrong. 'He said Justin had been in an accident and I immediately thought, *Oh my God, maybe he's broken his legs*. But he said it was really bad and that Justin was in the neurology hospital.' Paula called her mother, who worked as a nurse. When Paula told her that Justin had been taken to neurology, her mother started to try to prepare her daughter for what was to come. 'She knew he didn't have much chance of coming out of the other side, so on the Tube she was trying to tell me, "You know, he might not be awake when you get there." That was a shock because then I knew it wasn't just a broken leg.' At the hospital, Justin wasn't conscious, but the extent of his injuries wasn't visible. 'He'd gone out of the windscreen, head-first, so all the trauma was to the back of his head. You couldn't see it when he was lying down. His dad kept telling me to talk to him, but I just didn't know what to say.'

No one had told Paula exactly what Justin's prognosis was. She was confused and in shock. As her mother left the hospital, she sat down with her daughter to tell her what would happen and advised her to stay the night. 'She was very honest with me and told me he wasn't going to wake up. Coming from the medical world, she must have been used to having to deliver that kind of news, but it must have been hard to do it to her own daughter.' Overnight, Paula stayed by his side, along with Justin's best friends and brother. At one point, she ran to the toilet to throw up and started to panic. 'It was all too much. Justin's mum said to me recently that she wasn't sure she'd done the right thing by getting me to come to the hospital. Maybe it was too traumatic for me. But even though it was, I think I'd prefer that to just getting a call to say he was dead. At least I had 24 hours to semi-wrap my head around it. Even when they turned the life-support machine off, you have this moment of thinking, *He's going to pull through*. But before then, I'd already had a moment of holding his hand and suddenly thinking, *He's gone. Like, I don't feel him in the room*. I felt he'd already gone.'

Paula went back to school a week later, and she finished her A levels. As she describes it, 'I just kept going. Kept going and going. I went to uni and I never came back.' In the immediate aftermath, she felt confused and scrutinised. 'We went to the crash site afterwards and there were loads of people there. One of Justin's ex-girlfriends, and we were only 18, but she was there wailing and crying. I thought, *Do people think I should be doing that? Should I be showing more?*' In the summer before university, she would wind up the windows of her car despite the heat, because she didn't want to feel watched. 'It's not like I had blacked-out windows,' she laughed. 'But I felt like people couldn't look at me if the windows were up. I thought if they saw me, they'd think, *What's she doing out? Shouldn't she be at home crying?*'

The sensation was heightened when on a normal night out with friends, just like any other 18-year-old. 'I went out with my friends one night and I remember feeling bad for having a night out. I felt like I couldn't laugh. I thought people would see me laughing and be like, *What's she laughing about? Her boyfriend's just died*. I worried that people wouldn't think I was sad enough, so I used to go to the cemetery every day. My dad thought it wasn't hugely healthy, but I felt guilty not [going].' At the same time, she could sense some people thought she shouldn't be grieving heavily. 'My headmaster said something to me like, "You know, you're 18, it's only your first boyfriend, you wouldn't have been together for the rest of your lives anyway." Looking back, he probably didn't know what to say and had never had a pupil go through that before. But the way he spoke made it feel insignificant, like I was making too much of a big deal about it.'

At university, Paula convinced herself she was fine. 'Every year, I'd think, *Wow, aren't I doing so much better now?* I wasn't doing well. I either slept all the time or stayed up all the time.' She sought out relationships to try to replicate the kind of young romance she'd had with Justin but struggled when they advanced. 'With guys, I was so desperate for a replacement, I'd get into something and then be like, *Oh God, the last thing I want is for you to actually come near me.* Justin and I were only 17. We'd listen to music at his house or go to the cinema. You'd hang out with friends or go to Pizza Express if you were lucky, but you wouldn't go on dates. And in terms of the physical side, it was all very minimal, because you're 17 and it's all very new. So at uni, it's meant to be this free-for-all, but I felt I just desperately wanted that connection of my best friend and putting on records and silly stuff. I stayed as a 17-year-old for quite a long time because in terms of relationships, that's what I wanted. I didn't want to be touched; I just wanted the comfort.'

Did she feel guilty about dating new people? 'No,' she says. 'It was at home that I felt the guilt, that I felt like people were watching me.' She pauses. 'Yeah. Actually, maybe I did. Because I just didn't want to be touched. Even with my own mum, sometimes, if she tried to give me a hug, I'd be like, *Do not come anywhere near me.* With guys, I'd find myself in situations [where] actually, afterwards, I'd realise it didn't make me feel any better. It actually made me feel worse. In the moment, you're enjoying the comfort, but once it's over it feels gross. Even to this day, there are times [when] the idea of someone touching me makes my skin crawl. I've been in proper relationships and there will be times [when] they kiss me and, in my head, I'm screaming, *Get off.* I don't want to say it out loud, but I can feel myself tighten up and think, *I don't want you near me.*'

When Paula finished university, she threw herself into work. 'I was busy, busy, busy, all the time. I worked in the TV industry, which is mad. It's all highs and lows. It's perfect for someone who's going through something because everything is intense. You travel a lot, you're away a lot. You're around people all the time. I moved up very quickly because my whole life was working and socialising around TV. At 25, I started waking up in the mornings at 5 a.m. I'd wake up because I was about to be sick. I had major anxiety, but I didn't do anything about it. It's only when I moved up to being a director, where I had a lot more responsibility, that I started to find it hard.'

Paula recreated the intensity of her work in her relationships. She found herself in a vicious cycle of initiating something, then running away from it, only to want it back. 'I had so many relationships where I'd have an instant connection and fall completely in love. Then it would trickle on and once things were getting serious, to a moving-in-together level, I might take that step, but then I'd be like, "OK, now I'm putting you at arm's length because I don't know what's going to happen."' Paula was so scared of another sudden loss that it was easier to control the end of a relationship than to risk being caught off-guard again. 'The guys I've dated have done jobs that take them away a lot. I have always thought, *But you might not come back.*

Rationally, I know accidents happen and you have no idea whether someone is going to come back or not in any relationship or on any day. But for me, I feel that we've got close enough now, and I don't want to get any closer because I can't handle this again. It's a catch-22 because you want it and when you've got it you're like, *No, thanks*.'

What did she do when she started to feel that fear? 'I'd just completely shut down and just be a bit of a dick. Then I'd run. I'd basically end it and be like, "No, I can't do this. Sorry. Bye." Then the minute that person moves on, I'd be like, "Oh no, no, no, no, I want you, I made a mistake." Because I thought I was still in love with them.' Now, Paula recognises that reaction as grief. 'The pain I felt about the relationship ending was the exact same pain as grief. It felt like Justin had died again. Those things don't match. The reaction wasn't proportionate to what had happened. I just couldn't work it out.' I ask whether, despite rejecting relationships, she also found it hard to be alone. 'Definitely. I'm an only child, so I don't have siblings to call on when I'm feeling bad. After Justin died, I didn't feel that I could just say to any of my friends, "Can you come and be with me because I'm finding it hard to be on my own?" At uni, they're just new friends – you don't know them well enough to ask them to come and sit with you because you're in a bad place. The only people I felt I could talk to were his brother and his best friend, because they were in the hospital, too, and they're the only people who went through the exact same thing.'

I ask if any of her boyfriends had linked her reactions to her grief, as some of Kenny's partners had done. 'Everyone I've dated has been incredibly understanding, but I think they put it down more to anxiety and depression than grief. They've all known what happened to Justin, but I don't think they made the link. I couldn't articulate it myself, though. If I felt something and someone commented on it, I'd be really defensive. I'd say, "No, I'm not doing that, you're doing that." It was really childish. It's taken me a long time to understand that not every argument in a relationship is my fault, because I always thought, *I'm the one with these issues, I'm the one that struggles.*'

Things came to a head for Paula around the time the coronavirus lockdown was imposed. At work, she had struggled to show up. She was in a relationship with a man who was older and more mature, who wanted to help her with how she felt. They'd moved in together, but as the restrictions were imposed she was unable to stop herself from leaving. 'He was like, "What are you doing?" But I just couldn't stay. And then I was at home, in my childhood bedroom, during lockdown, and I realised, *I'm 33, and all I've been doing is running since this moment my boyfriend died, and it's all caught up with [me].* In lockdown it was suddenly like I had to sit with all that awful pain for the first time.' Paula started going to therapy and addressing her relationship issues. 'I realised that I was caught in this cycle of loss. I was with this amazing man who wanted to offer everything to me and all I could do was run. I could see I'd started causing more loss to myself because I was putting up barriers and pushing people away.'

Through therapy, Paula has managed to start articulating her emotions. 'I'm at a stage now where I can feel myself starting to want to run, and I can stop myself from doing it. I'm much calmer and I listen. I'll listen and then I can respond. Now I can understand when I'm feeling scared and that that's where the struggle comes from. Obviously, some people you date, it's not a vibe. But when it is a vibe, why would I be acting like this? There's absolutely no reason for me to be running away.

When I sit down and break it down, they've done nothing wrong. It's just that I'm scared because it feels like there's so much to lose.' As she's got older, the fear has intensified as the stakes seem higher. 'There's the added pressure of thinking about children. For me, the feeling is, *Well, what happens if I have children with someone and they don't come home one day because they have an accident?* It's always the barrier and the only way to break through it is to just jump.'

The impact Justin's death has had on Paula is clear. Losing her first experience of love so suddenly and so traumatically has altered her ability to develop more stable, mature attachments. The impact is clear in the contrast she sees when she looks at Justin's photos. 'I look at his picture and I think, *I don't know what that boy is. Who would he have been?* We were just starting our lives. We were just leaving school and going to university, where you start to become more of who you are as an adult. It's so far from me now. He's just a boy. My life has moved on, but I can't promise anyone that it's ever going to change for me. I can only do my best.'

Four

Dream Jobs

Success, ambition and returning to work

When my mother was ill, I threw myself into activity. There was always something I could be working on. On the S-Bahn in the mornings in Berlin, I'd fight for a seat so I could read. At work, I would oscillate between the tearoom, making umpteen cups of tasteless vending-machine coffee, and the translators' office, where I worked quickly to complete all my translations within the morning. I fiddled my timesheet and spent the afternoons working on a novel I had decided I would magically publish before my mother died. In the evenings, I'd take my laptop to a strange little café deep in Neukölln and order thick slices of cake and milky German lattes. I didn't need to worry about the caffeine because I barely slept anyway. I'd work on the novel, or on the freelance editing job I'd landed with a local magazine, who paid me by the word to correct English articles written by non-native speakers. I'd decided to write a screenplay, too, and still pitched articles to publications I'd written for in Melbourne. In part, my restlessness was a manifestation of millennial 'side-hustle' culture, which, for a time, had seemed so aspirational. But there was another driving force that ran deeper: anxiety. I'd realised that what I didn't accomplish now, my mother would never see. I was desperately running out of time.

When I received the call from my father that my mother's cancer had spread, I packed up my Berlin life overnight. I sent a text to my manager resigning. I'd never told anyone at work that something was wrong at home. I hadn't known when my mother's illness would become 'relevant' information. Since I was still in the probation period, I only needed to give a week's notice. I received an email from the HR manager as I landed in England the next morning demanding that I return my office key card, and saying that my subsidised lunch vouchers would be docked from my pay. 'Sometimes things happen in life, but we still have to follow protocol,' he wrote. My shock at his insensitivity flashed like acid through my chest. How did he not realise how utterly insignificant all that was? How could he be so fucking stupid?

That furious astonishment was emblematic of a change in my attitude towards work that lasted for a few years after my mother's death. Employment lost all its meaning for me beyond pure economic imperative. At 25, I felt I'd been doggedly pursuing *something*, though I was never exactly sure *what*, since going to university. I vaguely worked towards some big success, some validation, something to make my parents proud, something to give me an identity, a more comfortable living, more money, more followers, more (*any*) recognition. I had drive but no direction. Suddenly, all those competing objectives – the restlessness and itch and random ambition – were revealed for what they were: hollow. Work was futile. I had no desire to keep doing it. Besides, what was I going to do now I'd quit? Attend a job interview months after my mother's death? Start a new job and cry in the toilets every day? Worry about my grief becoming cheap office gossip? I'd learnt that half of succeeding at work was performing enthusiasm, day in and day out. In those early months of grief, I couldn't imagine anyone asking anything of me and being able to muster the requisite jolly compliance. My father encouraged me and my brother to go back to work as soon as possible. He believed it would be a good distraction, but distraction was the last thing I wanted. In Berlin, I'd distracted myself out of facing up to the fact that my mother was dying. It had stopped me coming home sooner. I wanted to let myself be carried away like flotsam in the sea of grief and to take the opportunity to enjoy what little pleasure was left in life.

I was lucky. I was able to get by for a year living cheaply on freelance jobs, savings and what I'd inherited of my mother's NHS nurse's pension. I kept thinking of the Annie Dillard quote: 'How we spend our days is how we spend our lives.' I wanted to spend them travelling, writing, seeing friends, music, sights. I used the year to finish my novel. I'd shown the manuscript to my mother just before she died and promised I'd publish it with a dedication to her, one day. If she had seen it, perhaps that would be substitute enough for her holding the hardback in her hands. Between the odd translation project and editing for the German magazine, I was able to enjoy the pristine London summer. After my flatmates had gone to work, I would head to a café for an iced latte, do a little work, then sit and read in the park. My mother loved the sun. Every time I turned my face to the sky and watched the darkness behind my eyelids dance into vivid red, I thought of her tanning her clavicles in the garden, her old summer dress hitched over her knees. Berlin had been bitterly cold and filled with the restlessness of anticipatory grief. Now, in the sun, I felt, for the first time in over a year, a sense of calm. I was torn and lost and desperately sad, but I no longer felt so anxious. The time had run out. I had the rest of my life to recover and I wanted to take my time.

When I travelled to Melbourne later in the year, I realised for the first time in my life that happiness, joy and fun were not frivolous pursuits. Before then, I had viewed them as 'treats' that were earned only through hard work and success. Talking to my therapist, I told her I suddenly realised that pleasure and contentment were *substantive* rather than superficial. They were an essential part of life. Happiness was not some fleeting emotion that somehow had less meaning than its heavier counterparts of despair and sorrow. I suddenly felt I truly *deserved* the good times when I experienced them. Happiness was meaningful because I knew it was what my mother had always wanted for me. Being guided by pleasure, rather than success, allowed me to somehow connect to her legacy, while giving me the space to process what had happened in that dark year I'd spent racked with the fear of her death. I woke every morning to the creeping memory that she'd died. I remembered I was grieving, and that was my task. That was what I was 'doing' every day. Looking back, I know if I had been any older or in a job I enjoyed, I wouldn't have taken the same amount of time off. I would have had more commitments that meant I simply couldn't afford the break. But I believe that the time off was the bedrock from which I managed to rebuild and recuperate in the immediate aftermath. The way I processed my mother's death would have been different had I been forced to return to work shortly after. Instead, the space allowed me to acknowledge the extent to which her illness and death were the life-altering, time-stopping events they were. I was incredibly privileged to be able to do so; as we will see, it is certainly not the norm.

I returned to work a year after my mother died. It was my first job in London since the temp work I'd done in the summers off from university. I could walk to work from where I lived in Hackney. I watched the comings and goings of East London creatives and long-time residents picking up their pastries and take-away coffees. When I walked home, I watched groups of friends meeting for knock-off drinks in the various pubs that punctuated the route. I was still getting used to the city after how violently I'd been uprooted from Berlin. I felt like I'd been washed up in London and wondered if it was too late for the place to ever feel like home. There was another feature to those walks in the first weeks of my new job. Every time I stepped out of the beautiful Grade II-listed building of my office into rush hour, I'd pull my phone out of my pocket. I'd unlock the screen and stare at the rectangle of blue light, thumbs hovering, as if I'd momentarily forgotten what I was doing. I'd realise that my fingers were navigating an unthinking impulse to call my mum. I wanted to tell her about my new job. I wanted to tell her about a compliment my new boss made about one of my ideas, or how a friendship was progressing with a new colleague. I couldn't do that anymore. As the weeks went by, I stopped automatically picking up the phone only for a new worry to emerge. Returning to work, my life had started to look 'ordinary' again. I was scared that my friends would see that semblance of normality as a signal that my life was moving on, and that I no longer needed their support. I needed them to remember that I was still grieving.

The first couple of months in my new job helped restore some structure to my life, but the novelty quickly wore off. Summer faded to autumn. The buzz of long, hot evenings subsided, replaced by the cold and rain, and the wet, dark crescents perma-soaked into the toes of my shoes. I had dreams about Mum. They were often harrowing. She was alive and, although I knew she was dying, I couldn't ask her about it or work out how I knew she was ill. In one dream, I 'woke' in the bathtub of my old family home from a nightmare in which she'd died. When I actually woke up, it was morning and I realised that the 'nightmare' was reality. I couldn't face getting out of bed. Tattered by fatigue, I listened to the morning traffic and sirens outside my window, and wondered angrily why anyone expected me to go to work ever again. But I couldn't call in sick. I was too embarrassed to ask for a day off, because I didn't want to have to give grief as a reason.

*

Grief is excellent at warping time. Fresh grief is particularly good at melting the rigidity of a calendar month. For that reason, a recently bereaved person may either enjoy the structure of work, which allows them to feel the rhythms of normality, or they may seek the opposite: to take the time to get their bearings again when their world has capsized. Society is not structured to facilitate that need. Bereavement leave is next to non-existent, on a global scale. Australia and Brazil grant grieving workers two days paid leave; Canada two days unpaid; China, France, New Zealand and South Africa up to three days paid. Workers have no legal right to compassionate leave in the United States. Similarly, in the United Kingdom, compassionate leave has no statutory footing with the single (and recent) exception of two weeks' leave for parents who have lost a child.

If a quarter-life griever has entered the working world, they will necessarily be junior. That brings its own challenges. The lack of seniority typically makes for a weak bargaining position. Young grievers will be unlikely to have the experience to assert their wish for time off, or bargain for more than what is offered under company policy, if anything is offered at all. They are less likely to have any savings to draw on to take any unpaid leave or a short sabbatical from work. And at the start of your career, any gaps in your CV can risk denting later prospects or slowing progress when other people of the same age are focused on progressing as quickly as possible.

Improving leave provision for bereaved people has been the topic of recent campaigning, its need sorely accentuated by the wave of death and grief brought by the COVID-19 pandemic. Rebecca Soffer is one figure helping to usher in change. The author and co-founder of the platform and book *Modern Loss* lost both her parents before her mid-thirties. She relied on her fast-paced job and New York lifestyle to distract herself from the grief. When I connect with her over Zoom, she is outside in the dappled sunshine of Massachusetts, where she now lives, wearing cat-eye glasses and red lipstick, her face framed by a mane of wavy golden hair. Her smile is broad and energetic, infectious even over video. When I ask her to tell me her story, she begins with the moment she landed her dream job.

Rebecca studied on the prestigious graduate programme at the Columbia Journalism School. In 2006, after graduating, she was hired as a writer on *The Colbert Report*, the first show to be helmed by the hugely successful late-night host Stephen Colbert. What drew Rebecca to political satire? 'I can't keep my opinion to myself,' she laughs. 'I was never going to be a straightforward journalist. I was hugely lucky to be an original staff writer on the show. I'd been in the job for a year. We'd just been to the Emmys in LA.' After LA, Rebecca went on a camping trip with her parents. She was 30 and felt like it was an opportunity to start getting to know her mother and father as people, rather than as parents. 'It was amazing because you're not 17 anymore, you're not arguing or falling out. It was a chance to reconnect, and I had an amazing time with them.' Her parents dropped her home in New York before setting off back to Philadelphia, where they lived and where Rebecca had grown up. 'I had this very inconsequential goodbye with them – hugged and kissed them – "I'll see you next week at Julie's wedding" – no big deal kind of thing.'

Rebecca still hadn't changed out of her camping gear when she got the call. There had been a car accident. Her father told her to come immediately. 'One of my friends was one of those freakish people who had a car in New York,' she laughs. 'He drove me like a bat out of hell to a hospital in New Jersey. When I got to my father's bedside, the first thing he said to me was, "I'm so sorry, Bec, she's gone."' Her mother had died in the accident. Her father had been in the car and watched her die. 'That was the end of my "before",' says Rebecca. 'I just remember thinking, *What do I do now?* I had absolutely no roadmap.' With no entitlement to time off, Rebecca had to return to work. She was thrown back into the high-octane world of late-night entertainment without any time to process her abrupt and violent loss.

'In the States, there's no bereavement leave. It's not a thing. I had to figure out what I needed. I didn't always get it at work because I didn't know how to ask for it. You know, I was embarrassed. I wish there'd been a structure in place to take care of me while I was flailing and trying to figure out my new reality. Instead, I dove into work and I went out too much. I just didn't want to be alone. I drove myself to the ground, getting really exhausted, because I just didn't want to feel.' Characteristically in cases of sudden death, Rebecca felt overwhelmingly numb. She allowed her work to consume her. 'In that first year, I moved very fast because I was traumatised. I had PTSD. It happened very quickly. It was a violent accident. I was in shock mode. My job sucked up my time. I ran 10-hour days. I had to stay tuned for the show; it taped every day, every night, Monday through Thursday. Dad was still in Philly, so I'd take the train home to be with him Friday after work, then come back Sunday night, maybe Monday morning, and go straight to the studio in New York at 6 a.m. Rinse and repeat.'

When the show went on hiatus for 11 weeks, Rebecca replaced work with travel. 'I kept buying tickets all over the world. I went to Venezuela, England, South Africa, everywhere. Travel helped. I felt better in unfamiliar landscapes while I was dealing with an unfamiliar feeling, but I really ran myself into the ground.' Coming into her second year of grief, Rebecca's numbness started to wear off. 'I'd done so well at work – I'd managed to get promoted in the first year [of grief]. The second year, though, was when I started to feel the pain and had to figure out how I was going to live with it. I started to realise, *Oh, this is a forever thing*. Like, it's every Thanksgiving, every New Year.'

Four years later, Rebecca's father died. By then she was married, and it was Rebecca's husband who broke the news.

Her father had had a heart attack on a cruise while travelling abroad. He hadn't survived. Rebecca was 34. She descended into heavy grief as she thought about life without either of her parents. 'We had all been so close. The loss of my mother was so incredibly incomprehensible. I still cannot even describe in words accurately what it does to your existence. It's such an incredibly existentially altering feeling, having this person – who's one of the only people who loves you unconditionally – vanishing from the earth. Then to lose your second parent and realise you have no one – that's such an existential crisis, especially when you're young. I didn't have kids. There was no one above or below me. There's no one taking care of you. At 34 – I know it seems old or like you're super grown up, but you're not; you feel incredibly small. I felt like a grief zygote. You're vulnerable. I wanted to build up a life, but how could I do that? The two people I assumed would be in all the pictures as I built it up are not gonna be in them. How do you make a meaningful life?'

Following her father's death, Rebecca decided to put her media experience into a project designed to challenge what grief looked like. She co-founded the Modern Loss platform in 2013 with Gabrielle Birkner, whose father and stepmother had been killed in a home invasion when she was only 24. Modern Loss publishes stories on grief and grieving in modern times. It has also joined the campaign to have bereavement leave legally recognised by the Biden administration in the States. The president is no stranger to grief. In 1972, his wife Neilia was involved in a car accident with the couple's three children, Beau, Hunter and Naomi. Neilia died, as did Naomi, who was only one year old at the time. Beau died of cancer in 2015. Much was made of the timing of his election during the pandemic: *Rolling Stone* recognised that grief was the 'unofficial theme' of Biden's presidential campaign, while *TIME* declared him to be 'unmatched as America's Grief Counselor.'

A major voice in the campaign for better bereavement leave is Evermore, an organisation described as 'an emerging movement of concerned citizens who believe that bereavement care in America is broken'. It launched a petition to establish the first ever White House Office of Bereavement Care to tackle the 'unprecedented mortality crises of gun violence, death by suicide, overdose, and COVID-19' through a centralised bereavement-care strategy across government agencies. Such a strategy is needed. Grief is a public health issue, and one that has rightly been recognised by psychiatrists and grief experts as being at the centre of a shadow pandemic after the ravages of COVID-19. According to a 2012 report from the Bureau of Labor Statistics, 71 per cent of full-time private-sector workers were given paid funeral leave in the United States.[1] Part-time workers fared even worse: 29 per cent received paid leave, compared with 71 per cent of full-time employees.

Similarly, in the UK, there is no statutory bereavement leave except for the death of a child. Employers are not required to give workers time off following a death or even in medical emergencies. Instead, it is completely at the discretion of the company, creating major inconsistencies not just within industries, but within individual businesses. In 2022, the UK Bereavement Commission found that a third of adults said their employer had not supported them at all, or only a little bit, after a significant bereavement.[2] The Commission found a huge variation across all aspects of support, including culture, paid leave, time before returning to work and the amount of flexibility offered. Many respondents reported a lack of clear communication from their managers. There could also be cultural insensitivities. For example, Caribbean respondents found their employers ignorant of the cultural tradition of Nine Nights (which, as the name suggests, lasts longer than the traditional one-day Western funeral). Other employers failed to recognise the significance of certain bereavements. As one respondent stated: 'We have aunties and uncles. They're not blood relatives but they are equally as important to us as our parents. My uncle died recently; he was my father's best friend at school. My uncle walked me down the aisle. He was Muslim. He died on a Thursday and was buried on Friday morning.'

The Commission concluded that new legislation was needed to require all employers to have a bereavement policy. In addition, it recommended that statutory leave and pay entitlement of two weeks be extended to encompass all close relationships. The government is encouraged to publish guidance on minimum standards for bereavement-leave policies and best practice for large, medium-sized and small employers. In particular, education regarding different cultural practices is needed to ensure all grievers have access to appropriate levels of support. Building on the two weeks' leave for bereaved parents – a hard-won right that was introduced in 2020 after the campaigning of Lucy Herd, who lost her 23-month-old son Jack – special provisions are recommended for those experiencing pregnancy and baby loss.

An important feature of 'Jack's Law' is the ability to split the leave up. Parents may take portions of the two-week allowance anytime within the 56 weeks after the date of the child's death. This allows employees to take leave for difficult dates such as the anniversary of their child's death, or the child's birthday. When it comes to other kinds of loss, however, this is a need few employers acknowledge. Ongoing leave within the years following a death should become standard. When I returned to work after my mother died, I asked for the time off on the anniversary of her death. Although my employer allowed me to take a couple of days off, this came out of my annual-leave allowance. I thought sick leave would have been more appropriate, in the absence of compassionate leave being offered. After all, the deathiversary is hardly a holiday.

Experts I spoke to confirmed that flexible leave should be part of employers' bereavement policies. Time off immediately after a death plays a purely logistical role: it gives the worker time to plan or attend the funeral and little else. The allowance must also encompass the employee's need to process grief. 'Two weeks is better than three days,' says Hope Edelman, 'but it's hardly adequate for the distress you feel. It's impractical to say "take three months" in a capitalist system, but there could also be better support on site in places.' This was another recommendation from the UK Bereavement Commission: employer-supported access to bereavement professionals and internal support networks. Emily Cummin, the co-founder of bereavement support app Untangle, agrees: 'There needs to be a better understanding that time off doesn't need to be all at the start. Some allowance needs to be kept back for the ongoing process of grieving, when it hits you after the funeral has finished and the support around you tapers off.'

The lack of adequate leave affects people unequally. Sue Ryder reports that low-income workers are at a higher risk of experiencing persistent grief, owing both to the higher impact of financial losses after a bereavement, and the higher barriers they face in accessing resources to help them cope with grief. Research and anecdotal evidence show that the security of knowing that leave is paid gives people the space and time to come to terms with the death. Even then, policy is not enough. Workers must feel confident that their employer will not penalise them if they actually *take* the leave.

Reformed bereavement leave is not just an empathetic nice-to-have. It is also economically advantageous. Better leave provision would pay dividends on multiple fronts. Where grief is unresolved or unprocessed, it will engender deeper mental and physical health issues down the line. An oft-cited study by the Grief Recovery Institute estimates that American employers lost $75 billion annually owing to issues related to unresolved grief.[3] In 2020, the Sue Ryder charity found that workplace grief costs the UK economy £23 billion a year through reduced tax revenues, increased use of the NHS and social care resources.[4] That's not to mention the employee loyalty that can be fostered through generous bereavement provisions. As is the case for many unaddressed health crises, investing in adequate bereavement leave may appear to give something for 'nothing', but would result in significant savings in the long run.

The absurdity of the lack of statutory bereavement leave is best illustrated when comparing the leave granted when life ends with the leave granted when life begins. Maternity leave is, of course, not directly analogous to grief. It is also imperfect and comes with its own debates (including the discrimination maternity leave can engender, and the fight for equal paternity leave). Yet maternity leave illustrates the way in which workplaces can and do acknowledge the impact of a life-altering event, and the sheer amount of time needed to process and adjust. Why not allow a similarly significant period of time to adjust to a significant death? As is the case with maternity leave, not all workers will opt to take the same amount of time off.

However, even knowing it's an option can sometimes lessen the feeling of panic and hopelessness many feel when pressured to go back to work too soon. As paternity leave aims to balance out the discrimination that can occur when a woman takes maternity leave, so too could a statutory entitlement to paid compassionate leave help ease the inequality faced by workers who cannot afford unpaid time off. More generally, significant statutory leave would help re-normalise the protracted experience of processing grief, making it something we expect, rather than something we censure.

*

For young grievers, the impact of grief on their working lives is not just a short-term issue. It can alter their outlook or approach to work over their careers. Just as we have seen how the fear associated with grief can impact our relationships, it can equally interfere with how much we dare and strive in our careers. 'If fear is not processed or acknowledged, it ends up creeping in and affecting many different areas,' says Julia Samuel. 'With work, that could mean staying in a stable but unfulfilling job because you are too scared to make a career change or leave a job you're unhappy in. It can affect your ambition because you prefer safety over taking risks.' Young workers already struggle with wage stagnation and a lack of job security. The added impact of grief curtailing their ambition was clear at meet-ups. Speaking to young grievers, many talked about their sadness that while their friends appeared to be focused on progressing or securing promotions, they felt that all they could focus on was simply getting through the day. Finding a fulfilling line of work was less of a priority than finding positions that offered some level of security, or were not too taxing, so they had room to process their grief.

This was the case with Amin. Amin's younger sister Leila took her own life, after years suffering from an eating disorder. She was 20 and about to start her second year of university. 'I had always worried about her because she was in and out of hospital for stretches at a time,' he says. 'I knew that the disorder could kill her eventually, but I never thought it would come to that. Mum and Dad did everything they could. I definitely never thought she was at risk of doing that to herself.' It was only subsequently that Amin learnt that the leading cause of death in those suffering from eating disorders is suicide, with complications from the disorder being the second most likely cause of death. He remembers his sister as sweet and childlike. 'She was sensitive and quite shy, although if you annoyed her, she had a temper. She liked things to be the way she liked them to be, so I could wind her up a lot by messing with her stuff as a kid. It's something I still feel guilty about now, because we never quite got the chance to change that dynamic.'

Amin had graduated from university and managed to land an internship at an online sports magazine. Despite his father pushing him to go into a profession, Amin was 'sports mad'. 'I used to wind my mum up by constantly having the football on. I nagged my parents so much when I was younger to get Sky Sports so I could watch the games. I loved it. I loved the stories of the players and the teams. There was so much passion in it for me. Dad never really saw it that way.' His father, who was born in Iran, was a devout Muslim who disapproved of the culture around sports. 'Sports isn't prohibited in Islam, but when I was growing up, the stereotype of a footballer was the pissed-up, unfaithful, flashy guy who used prostitutes and drove around drunk. He saw it as idol worship. That behaviour wasn't what my father wanted me to aspire to. As an adult, I understand it came from a place of wanting what he saw as "the best" for me, but our views on that when I was a teenager just didn't align.'

Amin remembers vividly getting the phone call. 'It was a Tuesday evening. I had just filed a short piece I'd pitched,' he says. 'I was buzzing. I think it was the third or fourth thing they'd let me write and I loved that feeling of logging on and seeing my by-line.' He was about to leave the office with some of the other writers to get a drink. As soon as he picked up and heard his mother's voice, he knew something was wrong. The details of what happened next are difficult for Amin to remember, and those he does he finds too difficult to talk about. 'In Islam, the burial is quick. There was some argument between my mum and dad because traditionally, women don't go to the burial. Mum wasn't having it and I'm glad she was there because I know she needed to be, but it was stressful for there to even be an argument about it. You've just learnt that this person you love has died and the next thing you know, you're there saying prayers and they're in the ground. I remember very little from that day.'

Amin only took time off for Leila's funeral. He didn't know what else to do except to keep going to work. 'I was in complete shock, completely numb. I went back in even before the end of the week. I remember seeing [that] my article had been published and it was like looking at something I'd written five years ago.' The office became a respite from the heavy atmosphere at home as both his parents grieved their daughter heavily. 'Mum and Dad both just became recluses, in different ways. Dad sort of shut himself away in his religion. He became far stricter than he had [been] before. Mum was distraught and she stopped leaving the house for a while.' Amin was worried about his mother in particular, who was inconsolable. At the same time, he craved her comfort. 'I felt like I'd lost them, too.' As protective as he felt towards his mother, he also felt resentful. 'She made it clear she thought her loss of Leila was worse [than mine], because it was her child. That was the same when I would tell people about my sister dying. Their first question was often about my parents, rather than how I was feeling.'

Amin's internship came to an end. He hadn't yet been able to find a full-time job in journalism. The industry seemed impossible to break into without doing a postgraduate degree, which he knew his father wouldn't support. 'It was like that was it. My dad very much had the attitude that I'd had my time to do my hobby and he had taken to asking me constantly what the plan was now. As his son, I was supposed to be successful and respectable.' Feeling worn down and directionless, and still reeling from the loss of his sister, Amin felt he had little choice but to pursue law. 'It was that or become a doctor, as far as Dad was concerned. I'd spent too much time in hospitals with Leila to want to ever go back to that or deal with death. So I chose law.'

Amin was disillusioned with his choice. 'I basically became a chubby stoner,' he laughs. 'And I was very good at hiding all that from my parents, because they weren't paying me much attention anyway.' Amin became depressed: he'd lost his sister, and his parents, and now he was giving up his dream career. His grief was complex. Suicide is still taboo across many cultures. It is prohibited in Islam, just as it is in Christianity. His parents battled with a deep sense of shame and found themselves misunderstood by members of their community and extended family. 'Some of my relatives made it clear that they thought

Leila had been insane,' he said. 'Other times, they just dismissed it as God's will, or said it was fated to happen. Those remarks were so diminishing for my mother, as if she should just be able to brush it off.'

He tried to help his parents understand that Leila's death was not a choice she made freely. 'I think generationally, I was a bit more willing to educate myself and try to understand what Leila had done. I read a lot about mental health – things I'd never been interested in before. I wanted them to know, from what I was reading, that Leila suffered an illness, just like if she had epilepsy or leukaemia. She hadn't acted with a sound mind. She was desperate. But it took a very long time for us to frame it that way. I think they still struggle with guilt now.'

Amin qualified as a lawyer. He hated his first few years. He was given a high workload of menial tasks. He felt that the law firm partner he worked under did not respect him. 'In hindsight, doing all of that bullshit admin work they make you do as a very junior associate was probably good for me. I wasn't in a good place mentally and, actually, that level was all I could handle. It meant I didn't have to think too hard. I hated the rigidity of it in comparison to being at the magazine, but it also made it quite easy to coast.' It was near the third anniversary of Leila's death that he began to experience panic attacks. 'I would be in a meeting or at my desk and I would feel a wave of terror. I felt like I was going crazy.' Luckily, one of the other associates recognised Amin's symptoms. 'She'd suffered anxiety as a teen-ager and she knew what was happening. She would come with me into the stairwell and sit and help me breathe and help me remember I wasn't dying.'

With her support, Amin was able to access a counselling service offered by his firm. In his sessions, he realised that he felt overwhelmed with guilt and self-recrimination. 'It wasn't just that I felt guilty about Leila, although I did. I hadn't helped. I thought Mum and Dad had a handle on it and so many times I wondered, *If I had been more involved in her treatment, would that have helped? Would she have gotten better?* And I wasn't that involved because I resented her. Dad preferred her as a child. She was more well behaved and willing to please. Dad always talked about what a success she would be. I felt like a disappointment by comparison. That was another part of the guilt. I was the remaining child and I felt as though I wasn't the one they'd have chosen. It was up to me now to make them proud. I had to do what she was supposed to do: be the good child and be successful.'

As he made progress in his counselling sessions, Amin began to make more progress at work. A turning point came when he was brought onto a case involving a sports agent and his client's football team. 'I loved it. I could finally connect with what was happening and what the issues were. Even though I still wasn't at the level where I had a huge amount of responsibility, I was actually engaged and invested in the outcome.' He managed to put himself forward for more sports-related matters as they came in, developing a niche. 'I found that being able to work in sports law helped me connect back to what I was passionate [about] before Leila died. Part of the old Amin can live on, in a way. And, actually, I get some of the same perks I might have got if I'd been a sports journalist. I've been given amazing tickets to watch matches at Wembley. One time, I got to see the finals at Wimbledon. I play in a five-a-side team on the weekends now, because my counsellor said exercise was good to help with my mental health.' Still, he finds himself feeling held back. 'Last year, I was offered a secondment in New York. I should have taken it, if I'm honest, but when I thought about needing to get to know a new city and new people and the pressure of that, I just wanted to stay where I am. There has been so much change, particularly with the pandemic, too, I felt like I just had to cling on to the one aspect of my life that's predictable. It took so long to find my feet at the firm and I'm finally doing work I enjoy. I didn't want the upheaval.'

His parents are still a concern. 'I didn't want to be too far away from them.' Their relationship is slowly changing. 'I think there will always be some pressure from my father. It's gotten less now that I am doing this job. He's getting older and some-times I think the fight that's in him has just quietened a bit. And I'm older. I'm old enough to see that the pressure he puts on me is an expression of his grief and his pain. He lost his little girl and I know he has carried a lot of guilt over that. But I know I will never be Leila and I can never replace her. I'm re-learning who Amin is outside of all this. I'm hoping the next time an opportunity like New York comes up, I'll feel grounded enough to take it.'

*

While some young grievers find that grief holds them back in the workplace, others plough into their work in order to cope. Feverish proactivity of this type can reap many rewards. Yet, time and again, young grievers report the inability to enjoy their successes purely. New achievements can, for a long time, feel tinged with regret that the deceased is not there to share in them. This was clear when I spoke to Joss Hogarth-Meek. Joss is a partner at Wired PR, a music publicity agency founded and created by Joss's business partner Rachel Campbell. Wired represents an abundance of cutting-edge, critically acclaimed artists such as Chase and Status, AJ Tracey, Ibeyi and Central Cee. Scroll through Joss's Instagram and you will find snapshots of the glamorous life you might expect of someone working in the music industry.

Joss's journey was, however, far more complex than the enviable highlight reel might suggest. When we speak, she is calling me from the up-and-coming neighbourhood of Acton in West London. She lives there with her husband in a house she owns through shared ownership and is proud of owning. That she is on the property ladder is made more meaningful by the fact that Joss spent two years living in a homeless shelter while her father was dying from complications related to alcoholism when she was 27. Her father had been a successful property developer. When she and her siblings were still young, he made a bad investment, and the family's once-comfortable existence turned into one of financial hardship.

Was the loss of financial stability the trigger for her father's drinking? 'No. He was always a heavy drinker, from even before I was born,' Joss says. 'It'd gotten really bad by the time I was about four or five, but he started to get severely ill from it when I was 16.' Despite their change in circumstances, Joss's father worked hard to make sure she and her siblings' needs and wants were always met. Born in 1949, he saw himself – like many men of his generation – as the provider and put himself under serious strain and financial debt to make sure he could still give his children what they wanted.

Joss was an energetic teenager. 'I was an absolute wriggler,' she laughs. She would subsequently be diagnosed with ADHD at the age of 30. At school, she recalls being considered fun – someone friends would go out to parties and gigs with. 'At the same time as being this fun, outgoing person, I was going through a lot. We were really lacking in money and Dad was in a world of debt.' She was obsessed with music; she dreamed of becoming a music journalist and starting her own magazine. Her music tastes were broad. 'I loved Task Force, Wu-Tang, but was a total Coldplay stan at the same time, Amy Winehouse … I loved lots of different things.' When she was 12, Joss's family moved from Somerset to London, allowing her to go to multiple gigs a week. 'I was out a lot. If I had a really good night, I'd want to relive it immediately with the people I'd met that night. I was, and am, definitely an addict's child in that sense; I'm always chasing a high. At school, I was always anxious to do things right away. That's the kind of energy I brought into my career.'

Music provided Joss with excitement and escape when she was facing difficulties at home. As she left school and began trying to find her 'in' to the music industry, Joss's father's health began to decline drastically. 'I'd always been an absolute daddy's girl. He was my go-to parent. He made sure I had what I needed. He was a really, really wonderful dad, even when he was unwell.' Her early memories of him are full of warmth and the feeling of being held. 'It's always key for me to say he was never abusive or violent. He didn't drink-drive. There were times he was supposed to pick me up from a friend's house or drive me to a gig, and he couldn't.' Joss saw his alcoholism less as a choice and more as a 'demon' that took over him. 'I didn't see it as him making these choices.'

When her parents split up, Joss's relationship with her father took on a new dimension as she found herself caring for him more and more. 'It had always been Mum looking after him. She kept the family running and together. I took over that role quite early in life.' Like many of those bereaved at a young age, Joss experienced an accelerated sense of responsibility that 'just grew and grew'. She conducted herself with pragmatism, an outlook that is still palpable when she talks about her father's illness now. It is clear she wants to tell her story not as a means of catharsis, but in the hope that it will help others whose loved ones are struggling with addiction to feel less alone.

Joss moved out of home at 18 and spent stints living with friends or their parents before spending time living in a homeless shelter. After a few years, she landed an internship that she thought might finally break her into the music industry. She worked hard in the role, but by this time Joss had become her father's primary carer. He was suffering from liver cirrhosis, a condition characteristic of alcoholics, and he needed more frequent medical attention. The stress of work, caring for her father and the precarity of her living situation somatised. Joss became seriously ill and was forced to give up her internship. 'I had a form of chronic migraine that affected my balance system. Looking back, I realise it was the result of extreme stress. Giving up my internship was awful. I thought my chances of breaking into the industry were over, because I'd been trying to get into it for so long and I'd finally found my way in and I had to give it up. It really confirmed my sense that nothing goes right for me and the world's against me. I was in that frame of mind for so long because nothing ever went right.'

Even while sick, Joss tried to take up another internship. She didn't feel she could stay idle. It didn't go well. Yet in a stroke of luck, she met the woman who would eventually become her business partner. 'Rachel had just founded Wired and I offered to help, and she said that would be amazing.' Joss had never considered publicity before but took to the job instantly. 'It blossomed from there and we built the company up together. I was absolutely obsessed with the job. It was just what I needed to make me feel like something not only was going right in my life, but it was something completely within my control. Not only that, but I could help other people and help them to tell their stories and feel safe. That is the goal. Obviously you want clients to feel safe and like we've got their backs, and we're only putting them in situations they need to be in. In many ways, that's the exact role I played with my dad.'

While caring for her father, Joss used the business as an escape. 'I completely launched myself into work and became absolutely obsessed with working. I would go and work at the hospital when my dad was ill, and I would work until three in the morning and be straight back from nine the next day. It just became my absolute saviour. For me, there was this link between grief and being productive.'

Unfortunately, Joss's father couldn't share in her successes. 'When he was ill, he had Korsakoff syndrome, which is a type of dementia alcoholics get. So, he didn't really get what I was doing. He'd see people singing on the TV and tell people I managed them, but I didn't. He didn't really understand.' Like many young grievers whose parents' deaths were preluded by illness, Joss knew her father would die but still didn't expect it when it came. She was at a Major Lazer gig when the hospital called to tell her to come. She thought it was another routine admission and told them she'd be in on Monday. 'It's my one regret,' she says. 'He was in intensive care and they wouldn't let me in when I got there. That was new. I realised something bad was happening. It was strange because even though I refused to accept it mentally, physically I just knew. I started crying and I remember saying to someone, "I don't want him to die." I'd never said that to anyone before. I'd always been so strong-minded and in a mode of just getting on with it. I'd never shown that level of vulnerability.'

After her father's death, Joss moved to Ladbroke Grove, on the opposite side of London to where she'd been living. She consciously spent more time with new friends who didn't know about her father or his illness. In all that time, Joss continued to keep her head down and work. 'I was always a big dreamer and I never put ceilings on myself. I never thought anything was out of reach, except maybe being rich. Even then, I'd walk past big houses in Belsize Park or Primrose Hill where celebrities live and think, *That's what I want for myself.*'

The flipside to this fantasy world, she says, is that she expects certain behaviour of people even when they've made it clear they can't be relied upon. 'It's allowed people to let me down. But because of what happened with Dad, I'd created a narrative for myself that people always leave me. People don't stick around. I recreated the patterns of instability and dysfunctionality in relationships that I'd experienced being the child of an alcoholic. I pick people I have to care for, where there's always something in the way of them loving me purely or putting me as a priority. That's essentially what having a father for an addict is like: he loved me dearly, but there was always something in the way. There's always something stronger than staying for your kids. He couldn't quite quit drinking for us. He had to quit for himself, and he couldn't do that.'

Being so accustomed to the role of caring for other people and catering to their needs is doubtless what made Joss so successful in her career. It also means that being proud of her achievements is no straightforward thing. 'I find it hard when people suggest that my father would have been proud of me.

I don't know why.' I tell Joss I find the same thing. Even if well intended, those comments seem to miss the point. 'Yeah. It's like, well, he's not here to see it. That's *exactly* the thing that's shit about it. It's almost kind of annoying when people say that. I'm not sure I wouldn't want them to say it, though, and I'm sure Dad would have been proud of me. But I still find it difficult to hear.' On a different level, Joss's career was the escape she needed from the stressful and painful realities of her father's illness and his death. It gave her somewhere stable, something that felt more reliable. 'My job was a means of me getting away from that feeling of chaos and instability. It was a means of me pretending that things were fine. It allowed me to experience something completely new that didn't have any of the associations of illness or death. So, I feel it's kind of separate from him, in a way, which makes it difficult to imagine how he'd have felt proud.'

*

The successful person who's overcome a childhood tragedy is one of our culture's favourite stereotypes. Harry Potter springs to mind. That stereotype is also something of a statistical reality. *The Times's Past Imperfect* podcast hosts Rachel Sylvester and Alice Thomson found that of all Britain's prime ministers since 1721, nearly half had lost one or both of their parents as a child. Historian Lucille Iremonger crystallised this phenomenon as the 'Phaeton theory', postulating that the loss of a parent in childhood can forge a restless, fiery sense of ambition, which has since been supported by other studies.[5] In the States, nearly 30 per cent of presidents lost their fathers when young.[6] One early comfort I took when my mother was ill was finding out which celebrities had lost parents at a young age and still succeeded. I developed an unlikely affinity with the Kardashians, who were in their early twenties and late teens when their father, Robert Kardashian, passed away.

These statistics make me think of my friend Felix White, a founding member and former guitarist of the Maccabees and co-host of the wildly popular cricket podcast *Tailenders*. Felix lost his mother when he was 17 to MS. Felix and his brothers made a success of the band only a few years after her death. He has spoken at length about his complicated relationship with success. In his book, *It's Always Summer Somewhere*, he explores how being in the band went some way to 'replacing' his mother's love, his popularity giving him a new source of adulation. Yet the big achievements, like playing Glastonbury, always felt worse than he imagined, because he ultimately couldn't share them with his mum. When we talk, he tells me how most performers he knows have some form of trauma, whether a death or otherwise, that drives them to do what they do.

When the Maccabees broke up after 13 years, Felix lost the source of love that had sustained him through his twenties and into his thirties. The band's break-up made him finally confront the grief he had been avoiding since he was a teenager. 'Right at the end, the most significant part of it, really, is that when the Maccabees ended, it was the first time I really felt that my mum had died, as if it had just happened. It can be 15, 20 years later, and you feel like you're right next to it, or closer to it than you've ever been. It takes whatever loss to be brought back to the most significant one you're trying to escape. A lot of people who have suffered grief young are provoked into hyperactivity. I definitely felt that myself, this feeling of: 1) life doesn't last forever, and 2) a sort of complex denial where some part of my brain felt like if I went and achieved stuff and I brought it back, maybe she would come back.'

I had a similar experience when, in the year after my mother died, I occupied myself by writing that novel. It was the earliest ambition I can ever remember having, from when I was a very young child. When it was rejected countless times by publishers, I wailed on the floor of my room. When my mother had died, I'd thought to myself: *Well, my worst nightmare came true, so why not my wildest dream?* When my novel was rejected, I realised I'd believed my mother dying was the pendulum swinging one way – that worst nightmare – and the book's publication would be the pendulum swinging back – my wildest dream, turned to reality. For it to be rejected felt like an imbalance: proof that, like Joss had felt, the world was against me. The scales were off. I couldn't make of my life what I wanted; it was entirely uncontrollable, and the only certainty was more loss and disappointment. When I called to tell my father, he attempted to soothe me by asking, 'What would Mum say to you right now?' I couldn't give him an answer. In that moment, she felt further away than she ever had. I couldn't hear her voice. I could imagine the words she'd use, but they were simply a fact, rather than anything I felt, like sunlight failing to penetrate the darkness of deep water.

I ask Julia Samuel why grief messes with our ability to feel the deceased person's pride. 'In short, it's bittersweet,' she says. 'It becomes far more difficult to connect with the positive emotion, because it is also a reminder of negative ones.' To feel the 'would have' – that dreaded conditional tense – is also to confirm the loss. It is, she says, incredibly common, and should not distress the bereaved. It takes effort and imagination to cross the void, to summon up what they might have said or how they might have celebrated you. Sometimes your world feels so radically different and distant from the one in which they were still alive, it is a Herculean task to try to connect over the void.

The important thing to remember, whether a griever finds themselves professionally scuppered or bolstered by bereavement, is to look beyond the obvious. 'Success', whatever it looks like for each individual, can give the impression that the bereaved is moving on and coping well. We may even assume that it's somewhat heroic: that their success is a means of surmounting adversity, as if those two things are not inherently connected. This was a point I touched on when I spoke to Kenny (see Chapter Three: First Love). 'It just is what it is,' he said. 'I don't like to think of grief as something that I've overcome. Being a Black trans activist, those things I can feel pride at surmounting. But with grief, it's just something that happens to everyone at some point. And even if you cope and succeed, that's negligible when you think of what you've lost.' It's net bad, I suggest. 'Yeah, that's bang on. It's still net bad.' However grief interacts with a person's sense of ambition and success, the point remains that we must look past appearances to find out what's truly happening in their emotional landscape in order to fully support them.

Five

All My Friends

Bad friends, supportive friends and losing a friend

Before I was bereaved, I thought grief was a private issue that remained within the four walls of the family home. I could only imagine what happened behind those closed doors, but I thought it was probably intrusive to ask. I assumed, as many people do, that the best support a person would have would be their family. Had any of my friends been bereaved, that view might have been challenged – but they weren't, so it never was. I learnt the hard way that when a death occurs within your family, the remaining members are not inevitably there to lean on. The opposite is more consistently true. After all, they are dealing with their own grief.

This was a common theme among young grievers I spoke to. Mia (see Chapter Two: Leavers) described having to get to know her father more after her mother's death; Amin (see Chapter Four: Dream Jobs) spoke of the complex emotions of protection and anger he felt towards his parents after his sister's death. Emily (see Chapter Three: First Love) touched on how she could see the aftershocks of her mother's death in every member of her family. 'For my dad, he was losing his wife; for my brothers, it was their specific relationship with my mother they lost. We all had independently lost a relationship that was so specific to us. That's deeply complicated because you're experiencing this thing that you do share, but it is so unique to you. It invariably puts pressure on your relationships. It's like a bomb has gone off and everyone is on shaky ground. It impacts your family in a really knotty way that just depends on how your family is built.'

My mother was the glue in my family. As my brother, my father and I found our feet in a dynamic radically altered by that loss, my friends became my key pillar of emotional support. I could talk to them openly about the difficulties of the changing family dynamic, and the complex emotions of grief more generally. Some rose to the challenge more than others. One of my best friends, Nicky, was an unwavering source of support. She took the train to my hometown the morning that my mother died. We walked up to the top of the hill near my house, along a path I had always walked with my mother, and sat looking at the view and the smattering of yellow daffodils. There was a small hut selling coffee at the top of the hill. We bought drinks and I watched young children running around with their parents, like it was just another gorgeous warm Saturday in April to be enjoyed. I barely remember what we spoke about, but I do remember that I felt I could tell Nicky how I was feeling – the strangeness of everything; the darkness in my thoughts; the confusion and sadness, but also my hope and gratitude.

Not all my friends were like this. I hadn't told some of them through quirks of timing and wanting to retain some outlet where I could behave normally, as though nothing were happening. I also lost friends. Grief brings existing fault lines to the surface and exposes rifts that might otherwise have remained in the friendship's substratum. The way some friends behaved made me feel that my mother's death was no longer relevant. I found myself exaggerating what a terrible time I was having, so I could 'prove' that my grief was still a valid feeling. I often found it difficult to ask for help when this happened. It hurts when the devastation you feel is so obvious to you but isn't being acted on by anyone else. Even while I wanted friends to see me as someone they could still count on for emotional support, it was difficult for me to play this role, particularly when I felt that my grief had not been adequately acknowledged. I ended up feeling pressured to set my own sadness aside and perform the 'supportive best mate' role, when I had no capacity to do it.

Our friendships naturally fluctuate over time, particularly in early adulthood. Many people will experience the waxing and waning of different bonds. The best friend you made at uni shows herself to be unsupportive or unlikeable. The group of lads you know from school begin to disperse, revealing wildly different interests and values. The mate you were least close to can end up becoming your best friend. In today's culture, friendship can be even more fraught for young people. It's a trite observation that, in an age of constant online connection, interpersonal connection is weaker than ever. The loneliness crisis in young people has been compounded by the pandemic lockdowns and social media. In 2019, a UK study revealed that 88 per cent of 18–24-year-olds experienced loneliness to some degree, with 24 per cent suffering often.[1] This was further exacerbated during the pandemic.[2] In the States, suicide rates among the 10–24 age group increased by 57 per cent from 2007 to 2018. Black children were nearly twice as likely to die by suicide than white children, and socioeconomically disadvantaged young people were two to three times more likely to develop mental health conditions than those from a wealthier background.[3]

The reasons for loneliness becoming more prevalent in young people are many. Some are simply to do with life stage: in emerging adulthood, social circles change throughout school, higher education and the workplace. That represents an opportunity to form new bonds, but it can also mean losses of old bonds. Emerging adults also experience the very formative tension between feeling a need to conform in order to 'fit in', and the need to 'find yourself'.[4] There are more factors at play, however. Social media use is well documented to increase negative comparison between peers, fostering a sense of isolation. Academic pressure and poor access to mental health resources can compound the problem. In the backdrop to all this are macro-stressors such as the ongoing effects of the 2008 financial crisis and various economic crises since, rising income inequality and climate change.[5]

On top of a demographic shift towards loneliness, young grievers also face barriers in receiving support from their friends when bereaved because of the ongoing taboos and misunderstandings around grief. The UK Bereavement Commission found that almost *half* (46 per cent) of their respondents had *no* support from their friends after bereavement.[6] That is a staggering and deeply saddening figure. While some respondents identified their wish not to burden others as a reason that they did not seek help, others cited the deep discomfort they could perceive in others when talking about death and dying as a barrier. Many described feeling 'misunderstood, avoided and abandoned' by friends in the months and years following a bereavement, or simply that their friends had no idea how to support them even while wanting to. There was a particular stigma around certain types of death, such as suicide and COVID-19. Insensitive comments and the expectation that the bereaved would move on within a set amount of time heightened their sense of isolation.

All of this means that today's young grievers have an increased likelihood of feeling acute isolation in grief. With that in mind, it becomes clear how significant a role friends play in what support a young griever might have. 'The biggest predictor of your outcome when grieving is the love and support of others,' says Julia Samuel. 'Your path to healing in grief should be paved with people – with people who care about you and who you trust in all areas of your life. When love dies, it's the love of others you can take inside you to give you the strength to do the work of grief.' Indeed, the Commission found that the respondents who had received practical and emotional support from friends and their wider community highly valued it, stating that they could not have coped without it. Notably, a direct relationship was found between high levels of informal support from friends and family, and the griever seeking more formal support. For each additional type of informal support someone had, they were 1.23 times more likely to access formal services. However, the report also found that, for most people, receiving a high level of informal support will be enough to get them through their grief, avoiding the need for professional services altogether.

Unfortunately, given a young griever's life stage, their friends are far less likely to have experienced grief themselves. Whether they have friends with the maturity, education or empathy to be good support or not is the luck of the draw. While in most instances if a young griever had a friend who had also been bereaved, they found this a great comfort, it is not a hard and fast rule that one bereaved friend can support another. Just as two unique griefs can 'clash' within a family dynamic, the competing needs of two bereaved friends can cause tension. As we will see, the support a friend offers will never be perfect. There are no magic words or things that they can do or say to make the bereaved's grief go away. However, the intention to support and the willingness to sit with the young griever's pain without discomfort can make the world of difference.

*

I met George at work. He was a colleague in the new job I'd started in London, the year after Mum's death. Like me, he was quiet, but we soon bonded when we realised we'd grown up near one another and shared a love of mid-Noughties indie bands. We'd put on Bloc Party or Jamie T anytime we were able to commandeer the speakers in our small office. A couple of months after joining, he sent me a message over Teams saying 'mad props' for what I was doing with The Grief Network. His friend Bennett had died a couple of years before and it was helpful to know that something like the Network existed. Bennett's death shifted the dynamic of George's friendship circle – a close group of lads who'd gone to school together. George's feelings about their support changed once again after his father's death from COVID-19.

'Bennett was a bit of a maverick,' George says of his late friend, to whom he refers by his last name in British schoolboy fashion. We are talking over a pint post-lockdown, just as restrictions begin to lift. 'I met him at school when we were 11. He was very creative and always hard to get hold of. He liked being mysterious. He was part of our friendship group. We all had different relationships. Some of us were more strait-laced, some were a bit weirder. For me, he was always the closest to me in terms of interests in culture and things like that.' Was he part of George's love for indie bands? 'Big time. He'd come to my house and I'd transfer all my music to his iPod and vice versa. We'd talk about music and share things, which I didn't have with any of the other guys. We were in a short-lived band together once. We called ourselves the Ampersands because that's a ready-made logo right there. We only practised once. We did a cover of "Disorder" by Joy Division and a White Lies B-side called "Taxidermy". Bit niche. We never practised again but we still talked about it. He always wanted to do something like that. He was a dreamer, really.'

When the boys left school and went to university, a distance grew. While Bennett pursued art and film, George's other friends went into more typical careers such as medicine and law. 'He was quite dissatisfied with the status quo of going to uni, getting a degree, getting a job. He did history of art, but the well-trodden path wasn't for him. He had quite a few mental health issues because of it. When we graduated and he saw people ostensibly "making progress" – getting internships, jobs, promotions – he felt quite alienated. We all moved to London and he still lived at home.' George admired his decision not to conform. 'He was doing life the right way and holding out to do something he really wanted to do. He switched his focus to film. He was interning and doing cinematography. He spent weekends in his shed at home painting. Losing his creativity and his "edge" from the group when he died shifted the dynamic massively, because he was so unique.'

George got the call when he was in Cornwall, at his then-girlfriend's house, from one of his friends. 'It was Pete, who I'm not massively close to. I thought it was weird, like, *Why is he calling me?*' When a second friend, Sam, called, George realised something was off. 'He asked if I'd spoken to Pete and I said no. And then he told me, "Yeah, Bennett's dead."' He, like George, was only 25. His parents had gone away for the weekend. Bennett hadn't answered any calls or messages for four days. When his sister went round to their parents' house to check on him, she found his body in his bedroom.

At first, Bennett's parents told his friends he'd died of a heart problem. George suspected differently. 'It wasn't intentional, I don't think,' he says, 'but we knew he was doing stuff. Nothing mad, but he was big into sleeping pills. He drank quite a lot at the end. I knew he drank a lot of whisky at night. We all sensed it wasn't a heart thing. I read a lot about the mixture of Valium and alcohol, and how dangerous it can be. I always assumed it was that.'

A hierarchy soon emerged within the friendship group. Some of the boys 'owned' the grief while others were more passive. 'The squeaky wheel got the grease,' says George. 'The friends in the group who were most vocal and outwards with their grief got the support. We all kind of banded around them.' George thinks the imbalance began with how the friends discovered Bennett's death. 'Pete's family are close with Bennett's, so he was the first to be told and delivered the news to everyone. He was a key part of the funeral. I don't think him and Bennett were that close, and not in the way his family thought they were.' The rest of the friends were not as close to Bennett's parents. 'It was strange because I knew him so well, but they didn't know that.'

Another aspect of the hierarchy was the timing of Bennett's death. 'We'd seen Bennett together three times in the two months before he died. He was on great form one of the times, but the other two he was really low. We were having a barbecue and he was trying to get drugs the whole night. We were like, "No one wants to do this, what are you doing?" The other time, I'd flipped out at him because he was defending the Manchester bomber. It was the only time I'd ever argued with him. He was such a soft, lovely, peaceful guy, so I couldn't believe what he was saying. I was screaming at him. So when he died, I felt like we were a bit estranged. Whereas, on the same day, him and Sam had had these deep private chats. Bennett was feeling out of touch with everyone. I think because of that, Sam felt like he was number one and he grasped the narrative. Between him and Pete, it was clear from the beginning that that was how it would go. Everything – the news, the final decisions for the funeral, what was said – all came from those two.'

With his two friends 'owning' the grief of Bennett's loss, the remaining friends felt disenfranchised. 'Me and the other boys would talk openly about how Sam and Pete were taking ownership. We went to see The National at Shepherd's Bush and the whole time we were just slagging the guys off – "What the fuck? We're feeling this, too." Sam started going out with this girl and, on New Year's Eve, we were all together and there was a picture of Bennett in the room. We'd all taken stuff and Sam started flipping out, saying, "I can feel him, I can see him, he's here." And then his girlfriend started saying she could see him, too! And I was like, "Mate, you never even met him. What's going on?"'

The hierarchy affected George's ability to grieve and, in particular, his ability to remember Bennett in the unique way he knew him. 'I felt like the way he was being talked about was wrong. We all contributed bits to the funeral speech we did, but it was terrible because by trying to take a bit of everybody's thoughts, it just became like a camel is a horse designed by a committee. It didn't get the sentiment across. It was difficult to have to remember him in a way that other people remembered him, rather than the way that I remembered him.' Bennett's funeral epitomised George's feeling that the Bennett he knew was being forgotten. 'One thing that fucked me off is what we wore. For our Year 13 prom, we were all told to wear suits and ties. Bennett turned up in skinny jeans, a vintage suit jacket and a horrible yellow tie. He had an earring in and a cigarette in his ear. I thought he'd have wanted us to wear something bright to his funeral, like a paisley tie, something like that. Sam said, "No, it's disrespectful, we should wear black." I was like, "For fuck's sake, I'm not wearing a black tie. Bennett would have wanted the opposite." So I was the only one wearing a colourful tie. He would have wanted us to behave normally, not just "respectfully". If it had been one of us who'd died, he'd have gone mental, so that's what he'd have liked for us.

'There were some things that were good, though. He had a wicker casket, which he would have loved. On the night out we had afterwards, one of the guys got a hand job in a park. There was a girl who a few of us had hooked up with over the years and one of the guys ended up hooking up with her again. So all these funny things Bennett would have loved. The kind of stupidness and doing what we normally do.'

Two years after Bennett's death, his friends still didn't know the cause of death. Eventually, Pete ordered the death certificate through the council. It listed the cause as 'heroin toxicity'. 'I think it means any opiate toxicity,' says George. 'I don't think he took heroin. There was no paraphernalia in the room according to the inquest, so I think something just went wrong. Funnily enough, three months after we got the certificate, his parents reached out to Pete and told him exactly what had happened. It was really nice to finally know. At the time, they held it back because they were doing what they could to get through it, and we completely understood. It was strange not knowing all that time.'

I ask how George's feelings about Bennett's death have evolved over time, five years on. 'In some respects, I can't imagine him being old,' he says. 'I think he would have found happiness and done great things. He was very talented. But I think he found life difficult. He was so pure and positive and optimistic; I don't know how he could have coped with the pandemic, with Trump, the state of the world now. It's not that it was his time at all, but I don't know how he'd have been as an older person. I can't imagine him as an adult. I like the fact that he's always going to be 25 in my head.'

George's feelings have also shifted since the death of his father. It was early April 2020, only weeks into lockdown. I remember George mentioning that both his parents had caught the virus, but he said they both seemed like they were doing OK. A weekend passed. When I connected to our department-wide Monday-morning meeting, I could see that my manager appeared shaken. His face was awash with emotion. He announced that he had difficult news to share: George's father had died in the early hours of the morning. I instantly tried to think of other Georges at the company. It couldn't be *my* George. It couldn't happen to him. Barely checking that I was on mute and my camera was off, I slumped to the floor and howled. I knew I had to talk to George, but I had no idea what to say. It even crossed my mind not to say anything at all. After all, what could you say in the face of such a tragedy? I had to follow my own advice and remember that saying something was better than saying nothing. I mention this because even for me, someone who'd lost her mother and ran a bereavement support group, it was difficult to think of any words that could be useful.

'Dad had chronic lymphocytic leukaemia,' George tells me, 'but it wasn't something that was supposed to kill him for 10, 20 years. When he was diagnosed in 2018, he retired and volunteered for a charity. He was a big guy, but he played a lot of rugby and went to spinning classes. He had a lot of time left.' At the onset of the pandemic, George realised his father was vulnerable and tried to convince his parents to stay safe. Unfortunately, it took some time for them to realise the risks. 'Dad stopped going to work, but Mum didn't. I had to say, "Mum, if you're going to work, Dad's going to work."' George's mother caught the virus and, despite her best efforts to stay away from George's father in the family home, he caught it too. 'He was a bit of a man's man and suffered in silence; he wouldn't complain. It was at the time [when] we were being told the last thing you want to do is go to the NHS and put pressure on hospitals, so they just stayed home.'

When his mother sent him a video of his father, George could hear his breathing. 'In hindsight, he was doing terribly. It was that deep, horrible, rattly … He was breathing from the depths of his lungs. Really hoarse. If you saw it now, you'd think, *Fuck me, he needs to be on a respirator*. At the time, we thought, *Oh, he's still breathing, he'll be OK*. There's a line in a Billy Bragg song: "You were so tall / How could you fall?" That's how I felt.' The song, 'Tank Park Salute', was written about Bragg's father's death when Bragg was 18; he has spoken about how frequently his fans have felt helped and healed by it. George related to the sense of impossibility in the lyrics that his father – so strong and towering – could ever be brought down. Seven days after catching the virus, his mother and father went to bed separately as usual. 'He was sleeping in my childhood bedroom and Mum would check on him every two hours. He was really noisy because he was breathing so deeply. Then she woke up at three in the morning. There was silence. She was like, *Fuck*. Went into his room. And he was just dead. She called the ambulance, had to get on the floor and try to do CPR – all this stuff. But he was dead.'

George had been isolating in Cornwall with his wife and her parents, who were also vulnerable. He stayed in Cornwall for six weeks until his family were able to arrange the funeral. At the time, restrictions meant only George, his mother and sister could attend. How were those six weeks? 'Honestly, they're not easier than what's to come, but you have so little else to focus on except getting through the day. In a sense, it was kind of nice to be with my wife and her family because I got to think about things on my own terms. They were incredibly supportive of me in those early days, and since.' Unlike with Bennett's death, there was no hierarchy and George felt as though his grief was the main focus. 'My friends were mostly supportive, to begin with. I did feel the love of people coming through at first. It also gave me perspective as to why some of my friends had behaved the way they did when

Bennett died. I understood how crazy grief can make you and how you do all these things you don't necessarily know you're doing.'

On the other hand, the fact that they'd had some experience of grief made George feel they should have been better at supporting him than they were. 'Despite the initial love, they kind of forgot. And to an extent I felt like, you haven't even had the big one yet. I'm not excited for them to experience it, but when they do, I think they'll realise what it's like. Bennett's death was significant, obviously, but it's not the completely destructive one. I feel like they don't know what's coming.' Within nine months, he'd fallen out with one friend who'd insisted on going to the pub while displaying COVID-19 symptoms. 'When I told him he shouldn't go, he said to me, "We've all been through the pandemic, you know?" That floored me. I mean, yeah, we've all been through it. Everyone went through World War Two, but some people had a very different World War Two. I couldn't believe how quickly he'd just forgotten why that would be significant for me.'

I ask George if he thinks some of his friends' failure to support him has anything to do with the fact that they're boys. 'Probably, yeah. Initially after my dad died, I spoke to each of my friends. I called them to tell them what happened, and that was great. But that's probably as emotional as it got. The love was shown through gifts. They'd send panettone or a book to read. But there was also this feeling of: *You're a man, your dad was a man, you need to be a man now. You need to step up and support your mum and sister.*' Where did that come from? 'My grandma, Dad's mum, does it a lot. She expects me to pick her up and drive her places now, like he did. His mates saw him in me more than my sister. We look very similar. So there was an element of stepping up and being a man. And I was like, *No, I don't wanna be a man! I wanna be a boy! A sad boy!'*

At the time we are talking, England has had all coronavirus restrictions lifted for four months. The two-year mark since George's father died has just passed. People are back at work and in pubs, and barely anyone wears a mask on public transport anymore. Two years on from his dad's death, George describes feeling worse than ever, just as everyone – the public and his friends alike – appears to be forgetting what he's been through. 'When the pandemic was still going on and being talked about and debated, at least the thing that killed Dad was the main news item. It was still taken seriously. I got reminded of it every day, but it was nice [that] it was being talked about and relevant. As soon as everything went back to normal, it all hit at once. I got the sense that nobody had taken anything from that period. I know people did, but I'd see people resuming their wedding plans with the same massive, huge wedding post-pandemic that they'd planned pre-pandemic. I'd think, *Hasn't that changed you in some way? Do you not want something different now? Has this existential threat not made you reconsider everything?* I found it difficult to see the ease with which people returned to normality.'

His friends' support has tailed off, too. 'It's really not mentioned anymore,' he says. I ask what would happen if he tried to talk about his grief. 'I don't know. I definitely bottled a lot of things up and that's come out in my actions in the last six months.' George shared that his own difficulty processing his grief resulted in causing pain to people he cares about. 'I'm going to CBT now, which has been really helpful. I feel like I can talk to you about it because of your mum, and that's it. I don't think anyone understands and I can't make them understand

and I don't want to *have* to make them understand. I don't want to have to put that work in,' he says.

'One friend checks in to the point where he asks the question twice. "How are you doing?" And then, "How are you doing really?" Then he's done and he's kind of ticked it off,' says George. I ask him what would happen if he took his friend up on this prompt and told him how he was actually doing. 'To be fair, my friends would rally round me. It's weird because my real answer to that question would be: *Every day is hell and I want to cry all the time*. I don't think life's good. The truth is *so* negative that if I lay that on them, it's too hard. So I may as well convince myself I'm OK. If I did ask for help, they'd probably come through for me because they're good people. They're just unaware of the day-to-day.'

*

The writer Tiffany Philippou found the support she received from friends crucial in processing the death of her boyfriend, Richard, who took his own life when they were both 20 years old. In her book *Totally Fine (and Other Lies I've Told Myself)*, she explores her decade-long attempt to numb the pain of her grief in 'socially acceptable' ways. 'Suicide grief has an extra layer to it,' she tells me. 'It's very much centred around shame, at least for me, because you kind of feel a semblance of control. It feels like a more preventable death than other types of death. People debate whether that's true, but I think the reality is that you can't help but feel a lot of blame. On top of that, people are already so awkward around grief, but with suicide, that's even more awkward. People are far less willing to talk about it.'

Richard and Tiffany met in Freshers' Week at Bristol University. 'We spent basically every day together from then on.' In second year, they moved in together with their friends. 'So even though we hadn't been together long, we'd obviously been part of each other's day-to-day lives. We were completely in each other's pockets. That very much added to the blame I felt of, *How could you not have known something was wrong?* His death took me completely by surprise. It was only in hindsight that I could see the signs, even if I never expected him to die.' It was the summer after the couple had finished their second year. While Tiffany was visiting a friend in Durham – a trip Richard had asked if he could come on – he received a letter to say he had failed the resits of his exams and would have to leave the university. He tried to take his life the same day. He was admitted to hospital, but his life-support machine was switched off five days later. Tiffany doesn't remember many details from the following summer months or the immediate aftermath of Richard's death. Loss of memory such as hers is a very common trauma response.

'I was very young,' says Tiffany. 'All my friends were really young as well, and that was quite definitional. On the one hand, my close friends from home were amazing and just showed up. On the other, I lived at uni within a house of boys where Richard's death was slightly swept under the carpet. I think that's quite emblematic of how men deal with things.' At the same time, Tiffany's own inability to process the loss set the tone. 'I talked to my mother about it recently and she said that I kind of took the lead. She said I was sort of orchestrating it all and being quite controlling, so people just mirrored me, so I wouldn't say my uni friends weren't supportive. Since I'd had that special status of girlfriend, I think people very much looked to me to know how to behave.'

She recalls the moment her close friends arrived at her house after finding out about Richard's death. 'I was at home when they turned the life-support machine off. Three of my best mates showed up together and you could just see the fear in their eyes. They were so scared. They just didn't know what would be there.' Speaking to her friends about the experience, they told Tiffany that despite their nervousness at seeing her, 'once we came through the door we realised you were just the same person', and they relaxed. Tiffany feels herself welling up remembering the moment. 'I can visualise it now. You could really see the fear. But it's amazing. I could tell they were scared of me and how I would be, but they showed up anyway and they didn't really expect anything.' Over the coming months, Tiffany's close friends were constantly there for her, taking her to the pub, drinking and smoking with her until late and talking to her about anything and everything. 'They got used to [being] around me and my grief. They let me laugh and cry and whatever was needed. Considering how young they were, and what relatively easy lives they'd had up until that point, they did an amazing job.'

The dynamic was different at university, where Tiffany and Richard had shared friends. Her male flatmates would rarely speak of his death, although she still felt their expectations about how she should act as the 'widowed' girlfriend. 'I don't think men are socialised to be in touch with their emotions. It might have changed now, but it was definitely the case in 2008.' Though Tiffany found herself centred in the grief felt around Richard's death, she still questioned her own right to respond as intensely as she did. 'We hadn't been together that long, even though we'd really been quite dependent on each other for our social lives.' This was reiterated to her in the way some people responded. A friend on her course lost his father in the same year that Richard died. By the final term, they had both lost another mutual friend, too. When they visited the Student Office to talk about extenuating circumstances, the officer intimated to her friend that she felt particularly sorry for him. 'It was like my grief for Richard was just less of a big deal than my friend's [for his] father, or like she thought I was overreacting by being so upset by Richard's death.'

Tiffany also found it hard to navigate other people's expectations about how she should act as the grieving girlfriend. 'I got feedback in certain ways that I wasn't grieving correctly or playing the grieving widow properly. Someone at the funeral said that I'd "worked the room" really well, almost in a way that suggested I shouldn't have done.' Some months after Richard's death, Tiffany started to hook up with one of her male flatmates. 'That was quite controversial,' she said. 'Obviously some of my flatmates thought it was wrong. In the end, we had a little house meeting about it. Looking back, that was quite a sweet way to deal with it.'

Despite some of the complexities, Tiffany has empathy for how her friends handled her grief. 'I don't really blame them, or anyone else, really, for my experience. The reality was that I was just very isolated by it, and I created or orchestrated a lot of that isolation. I felt so guilty. I felt guilty for not having let him come to Durham, though he asked me so many times. What if he'd come? Would he not have died? I felt guilty for not picking up on the signs. I went over a lot of what else I could have done. It was all too much to deal with, so I just kind of didn't.' She can still feel, however, the resentment at having lost the carefree feeling of youth that her other friends were clearly experiencing. 'By the time I was doing my finals, our other friend had died. I just didn't care about my finals at all. I had friends at other universities who were so stressed about finals and will still talk about that time and how stressed they were. I still feel a bit bitter about it, to be honest. I felt robbed of that experience of being young.'

Without knowing how to cope, Tiffany relied on what she called 'socially acceptable' coping techniques. As a young person, this included drinking excessively, but also involved throwing herself into work. 'I worked at early-stage start-ups, which are already quite an intense work environment. I never had, for example, a proper line manager or any support. I think you're supposed to work hard in your twenties, because you have the energy to do it, but my relationship with it wasn't healthy. I ended up being treated as more of an adult than I was really ready to be and took on that stress at work. No one readily thinks it's a problem, though.'

Outside of work, she drank a lot with friends. 'To some extent, it was that era where problematic drinking was quite normalised. I still drink now but in a much more normal way.' Though Tiffany recognises that drinking to excess was unhealthy, she also sees it as part of the friendship dynamics that helped her to heal. 'You'd expect the narrative around my drinking to be bad, but because I was always surrounded by good old friends when I was partying more heavily, they were sometimes the only times I would actually open up a little bit. And it's a bit what your twenties are for. In your twenties, everyone feels like a family. We'd party all weekend and I'd have friends stay over in my bed and stuff, so it always felt like a community in its own unofficial way. I think if that grief would have happened to me now, in my thirties, when my friends have their own lives and kids and stuff, I think I would have been lonelier because in your twenties your friends are like your family.'

After years of failing to process her grief, Tiffany was finally forced to confront it. 'I had essentially a bit of a breakdown. It still felt, eight or nine years later, like it had happened yesterday.' This is another common trauma response – that the event feels like it's happening in the present, rather than in the past. 'At the time, I remember my mum said it was my past catching up with me.' Tiffany went to therapy and became far more invested in her wellbeing. She trained to become a life coach. Writing her book was, as she describes it, an exercise in confronting the shame she felt around Richard's death. 'There was a lot of self-development in that era,' she says.

Part of that self-development was rediscovering her empathy for other people's problems. 'When your friends are young and haven't had many difficulties, and you're grieving, it's obviously very easy to think that what they're going through is, relatively, nothing. Once I gave myself permission to begin to feel and engage with what had happened, it actually opened me up to be able to empathise with people's problems and accept [that] everyone's carrying different forms of pain. When you're in it, it's really hard to see through your own pain. But once you do, you have the gift of being able to bring that to other people's experiences and be more empathetic. So I'm more empathetic to other people's stuff, even if it's small stuff, than I may have been before grief.'

Fittingly, it was a friend who helped prompt a realisation that helped transform Tiffany's relationship with her grief and with Richard. 'I'd always hated birthdays. I can't remember the day Richard actually died, but I remember his birthday. His birthday was always a really challenging day for me and that was the only date I really had. He also died quite shortly after my own birthday, so I'd be quite weird about my birthday, too. I never wanted to celebrate a birthday because it felt wrong. And my friend said to me, "To celebrate birthdays is to celebrate life." That gave me permission to celebrate. It's challenging when days that are meant to be joyful are also really sad. But now I try to do what my friend told me to do. I try to celebrate life.'

*

Whether or not a griever feels supported by their friends can be dependent upon the attitude they take to friendships. Despite the abundance of advice that divides supportive behaviour into rigid 'dos' and 'don'ts', very often grievers don't have prescriptive expectations of their friends and do understand how uncomfortable it is for them. This was evident when I spoke to the director Freddie Waters, whose sister Florence died from hypothermia in 2018. She was 33. When we sit down to talk, Freddie prefaces the conversation with some apprehension. 'I don't speak about it a lot, so I worry I'm going to ramble … Could I surprise myself? Could I get really upset? I'm unaware of where I could go and the death itself is so complicated to explain, but it's quite relevant to how I processed it.' The worry of rambling is something I hear often. In fact, I think it's one of the things that often stops grievers from talking openly to friends about their grief: the stories and feelings are so complex and nuanced, they take time to tell. Sometimes, the best support someone can offer is simply to commit to the time to listen.

Florence suffered from Ehlers-Danlos syndrome (EDS). EDS is a rare set of inherited conditions that weaken the connective tissues in the body. Though there are various types of EDS, which affect people differently and with varying severity, symptoms typically include hypermobility in the joints and easily bruised or broken skin. Up until recently, EDS was not recognised on the NHS. 'Florence had been unwell for quite some time, but couldn't get a diagnosis,' explains Freddie. 'It took ages for her to work out that she had EDS. At the time, EDS was only recognised in America and Germany, not in the UK. People had told her she was anorexic or that she was making things up. There was a vicious cycle between her mental health and her physical health. By the time she died, she wasn't herself. It was a very unusual and complicated thing going on.' To cope with her deteriorating mental health, Florence had taken up an involved style of meditation requiring the meditator to practise outside in a single spot over a significant period of time. It is typically undertaken under supervision, but Florence would often meditate alone. 'It was really the only thing that tended to help her mental state,' says Freddie.

Florence had insisted on going to meditate the day that she went missing. Though Freddie and his mother had tried to discourage her, she was insistent that it was the only thing that would make her feel better. When Freddie checked on her in the morning before she left, he sensed she was not herself. 'She had a small bag, like a canvas bag that you'd take to do errands. She wasn't well, but it was difficult. We'd never had friction between us and we were really close. She said she had to go. And I asked, "You're not going to disappear, are you?" And she said that she wouldn't, so she went.' Worried about his sister's mental state, Freddie called his father for help. 'My dad wasn't in the picture much growing up, but Florence adored him. I called him to say, "Now's your time to make a difference." He called Florence's phone and a stranger picked up because she'd left it at the bus stop outside Oxford.'

Freddie knew this wasn't good, even though Florence was not typically great with her phone. The family reported Florence missing. News outlets picked up the story. 'The police said the press was good and it would help.' Over four days, the family anxiously waited as the police began their search for Florence. 'I knew from police shows that after 72 hours, it's never good,' says Freddie. The police finally discovered sightings of Florence. 'They found her body on the fourth day. She was lying down out in a field, twenty minutes outside Oxford. She'd got a bus out and was seen by people in the village. She had food and a toothbrush and underwear with her. She was planning to do this meditation, but it had just gone wrong.'

At the inquest into her death, Florence's death was ruled accidental. 'There was nothing to suggest it was suicide,' says Freddie. 'It's frustrating because some people ruled it off as that. But at that point, was she … had she maybe lost the will to live? Because she was so down? It's a complicated one. I don't think she meant it to happen. Before she died, she seemed to have entered this phase of wanting to start something new; she was meditating to try to get better. She drew a lot – she did a lot of art and was writing a lot. It was about new beginnings, not about her kind of coming to an end.'

As he finishes telling the story of how Florence died, Freddie takes a breath. 'Sorry. I feel like that's taken ages to explain already. But it's important because part of the grief is the trauma of those four days and dealing with that, because even the day before she went missing when she clearly wasn't well was traumatic and awful. What it does to a family and what it brings up. And then she goes missing and it's your worst nightmare – you're getting news bulletins about your sister being missing and dealing with the press and putting on a brave face.' I tell Freddie there's no need to apologise. How did he feel once he was told about her death? 'My initial response was just shock at how you carry on and the ability to laugh and still find humour. This is so silly but there had been footage of Florence shopping for food before going and she just bought this cabbage ...' He laughs. 'It's not funny at all. That's your sister the day before she dies, but we were all laughing together, my family and the police officer, about how random this cabbage was.'

Freddie's friends immediately rallied around him. 'A couple of days after Florence's body was found, my friends showed up at my mum's house in Oxford. Too many friends – like 15 of them. We went out for lunch. It felt nice that I had friends who would drop everything and come and be that supportive.' Freddie's friendships were already strong. 'Because of what happened with my family growing up, my dad not being in the picture and some other stuff, I have always had really close friends and a close support network. That's one of the defining things I feel about that time – how supported I was and how supported I felt. I never felt forgotten.'

I pick up on this. Did he not feel, as Amin (see Chapter Four: Dream Jobs) and others who'd experienced sibling loss did, that his grief was less recognised than that of his parents? Freddie shakes his head. 'No, I never felt that. But that may be because of the overwhelming support I got from my friends. I don't want to invalidate anyone else's experience, but that's not how I felt. If anything, so much of my grief was the absolute worry I felt for my mum. That was one of the main parts. My mum losing her daughter ... Being in a room with your mum and your [other] sister with a policeman delivering the news that they've found a body. Going through that with my mum, and what she'd been through with Florence's illness – that was so difficult.'

Freddie recognises that his and his friends' ages, in their late twenties and early thirties, might have made a difference in terms of their ability to show up for him. 'I can imagine the younger you are, the harder it is. I felt very lucky that it had happened at an age when my friends were mature enough to be able to communicate in a way that just feels good. I remember thinking, *Fuck me, doing this at 18 or 19, my friends wouldn't have been able to deal with it. I'd have been let down.* Some friends really surprise you and some of them, I thought, *God, you're way more mature than I thought you were!* I was really impressed by some of them. Others didn't have a clue, but I could sense that they were sorry. They clearly didn't know what the fuck to say, and I was like, "I get it! It's really weird. It's hard." I can see how easy it would be to get annoyed because you go and hang out with people after and it's like, *Are we going to acknowledge the fact that my sister just died?* But that's not my approach to friendship. I don't put those expectations on my friends.'

Freddie has hit on something useful to remember. Not all friends show their support in the same way, and having friends who can play a variety of different 'roles' is useful. Some can offer space to talk, others can offer distractions. Each way of 'showing up' is different but will be recognised if the intention is there.

Following Florence's death, Freddie's way of coping was 'to just carry on'. He went through a break-up and spent a lot of time at home in his flat in London. 'I put a lot of my grief into that relationship and feeling sad about [it] breaking down. I went to get this acupuncture therapy and I remember the whole time I talked about the break-up and not my sister dying.

Death either takes relationships one way or the other.' He also put in place more boundaries, socially. 'It teaches you that you can say no to something you don't want to do. I rejected a lot of invitations to things at the time and did the things I did want to do. But after a while, you realise it's only so productive to sit in bed watching TV shows all day,' he laughs. 'I got up and I carried on.'

As Freddie directs comedies, I am unsurprised that he picked up on how laughter can help us through the bleakest times. I ask him how he feels about the way grief is portrayed as something invariably dysfunctional and despairing. 'Yeah! Yeah, it's interesting. People dramatise their worst nightmare, rather than actually how you respond to grief. I was shocked that something so terrible could happen and I could still laugh. I was amazed at finding humour in the darkest times. It's really interesting and inexplicable what laughter is and how much [that] alleviation is about pain and masking pain. But to be honest, my reaction to grief would have made a fucking boring TV show. I just carried on and shot a film three weeks after she died and had a sense [that] I wanted to deal with it in my way.'

His connection to art and culture helped him not only to carry on, but to connect to Florence. He describes the classic dynamic of an older sibling shaping and influencing a younger sibling. 'Everything I loved and the tastes I have are all because of Florence. She introduced me to most of the things in my life that I like. She was the opposite of me in lots of ways – very smart and introverted and read loads. She was so interested in art, and the arts more collectively. Every time I watch something I like or see something I like or hear something I like ... I want her opinion on it. You'd go to an art gallery and so many people find it hard to articulate how they feel about a gallery, but she would just have an insightful way of summarising it. I always knew that would be how I connect with her.'

Despite 'carrying on' at the time, Freddie finds he is only just starting to feel connected to his grief and the sensation of truly *missing* Florence. 'For a long time, I had no joy in talking to other people about grief, but I think I haven't scratched the surface. In the last six months, it's only just started to sink in. Six months ago, if you'd talked to me, there would have been no way I'd have cried, but I've felt myself going a bit as we've been talking. My other sister got married recently and the night before I just cried. I was so sad that Florence wasn't going to be there. I went to Sundance Film Festival with Florence a couple of times and I was there again last weekend. The fact that I was going again without her hit me, where it used to just be a passing thought and I'd carry on. Last weekend, it was like, *Fuck ... am I really going to stop and have a cry about this right now?'*

With this new engagement with his grief, Freddie has found himself interested in other emotions he hasn't yet faced. 'I'm interested in guilt. It's such a cliché and I didn't let myself feel guilty because I thought, as soon as I feel guilty – which you do, straight away' – he laughs – 'I just kind of decided not to. I'm only thinking I need to explore it more now because I was the last person who saw Florence before she left that day. My interaction with her could have been different and perhaps she wouldn't have died. I know it's not my fault, but it is also directly related. I think I knew, though, if I felt guilty at the time, I wouldn't have been able to get up and carry on.' I tell Freddie I also had a moment where I refused to feel guilt, just after I'd got the call to come home from Berlin. I thought I'd never forgive myself for having moved there while my mother was sick, and wasting time I could have been spending with her. It felt like a door that opened and I refused to step through it: if I felt that guilt, I didn't think I'd ever come back from it. 'That's so interesting to me,' he says, 'because that's a situation where obviously there's absolutely no reason for you to feel guilty at all and you still did. It's reassuring to hear.'

As we come to the end of our conversation, Freddie returns to the importance of his friendships. 'I felt, and still feel, so rallied around and understood. It gives you perspective to understand your boundaries. You know when you will and will not tolerate other people's behaviour, even if they're going through something. It's helpful to weed out friends that maybe weren't really friends in the first place. I feel so much richer as a human being for going through it and wiser in ways that are profound and hard to articulate. The strength that comes with knowing, if the unthinkable happens, will I collapse or carry on? No, I'll carry on. I have the support there to help me.'

At first, after speaking to Freddie, I think he has one of the more enlightened attitudes to friendships of all the young grievers I've spoken to. I put it down to his and his friends' relative maturity, being in their late twenties and early thirties. But when I reflect on it, much of what he says was echoed by other people, if not with the same generosity. Most young grievers know when their friends are trying. Many have empathy for the discomfort their friends might feel. Many worry about over-burdening their friends or expecting too much. The disappointment comes when there is no acknowledgement whatsoever or when a friend minimises the scale of their grief. In those cases, though, this is often just a clarifying moment when someone who wasn't a best friend to begin with is simply revealed as a connection not worth having. Where friendships or romantic relationships break in the wake of grief, more often than not the fault lines already existed. Grief simply makes them intolerable.

Why is it important to recognise this? There is so much advice dished out to the non-bereaved on how to be a 'good friend' to someone experiencing grief. This advice is often reduced to binary 'dos' and 'don'ts', often drafted more with the intent of affirming a griever's feelings than offering guidance to a non-bereaved friend. I have seen these kinds of posts on Instagram and personally felt a satisfied, *Yes!* But how much does this advice encourage people to face their discomfort and step into that painful space with the freshly bereaved? I'd wager not a lot. In fact, it can do the opposite. It can make people so scared of getting it wrong that they don't reach out at all. Even people who've been bereaved themselves experience this apprehension. It's counterproductive to create rigid tariffs of advice, because each friendship is different and each friend can offer different support. I have learnt that the only cardinal one-size-fits-all rule is acknowledging the death and listening to the griever without judgement or diminishment. The supporting friend will get things wrong. But the bereaved will always remember those who at least tried, and those who didn't.

Six

Marriage and Children

Life transitions, parentless parenting and
the legacy of young loss

Growing up, I loved to look at my parents' wedding photos. My father was slim, handsome and wearing preposterously large eighties glasses. My mother was fresh-faced and elegant in a classic white dress, a delicate circlet of flowers crowning her dark-brown hair. It fascinated me that my parents had existed as these shinier, younger versions of themselves. A couple of the photographs hung on the wall in our dining room, while the full suite lived in a special leather-bound photo album my mother would carefully take out to show me. The soft colours and old fashions were a time capsule into a past I hadn't lived but knew I was integrally tied to. I imagined what my own wedding photographs might look like and who would be in them beside me. Once I got married, I knew I would want some children. Maybe a pair, a boy and then a girl, just like me and my brother. Or just two girls. Two girls would be better. Boys were kind of gross.

Implicit in these childhood daydreams was the assumption that my parents would be there, somewhere in the background, like my grandparents were in those wedding photos. Dad would walk me down the aisle when I got married and my mother would come to meet my newborns. Mum loved to tell the story of my grandmother arriving at our house when my brother was born. My father opened the door, only for my grandmother to push past him impatiently, without a word, heading straight up the stairs to see her grandchild. In the summer holidays, my grandmother came to stay for weeks, entertaining me and my brother with long walks and building tents in the garden while my mother went to work. I carried the assumption that I would have the same support available to me when I finally had kids.

I am now, as an adult, far more ambivalent about marrying and having children. (And if anyone was going to walk me down the aisle, I stroppily told Dad once when I was a teenager, it was going to be *Mum*.) As a society, we are long past the era when getting married and having kids are universal aspirations or norms. As is well known, younger generations are increasingly delaying these markers or opting not to do them at all. Despite this, many of us grow up imagining what these moments might look like for us, just as we dream about what we might want to do when we grow up or what we might want to achieve. When you lose someone, those unactualised images are drastically altered. On the one hand, getting married and having children would comfortably replicate and replace the cosy family unit I grew up in and subsequently lost when my mother died. If I have children, parts of my mother will live on through her DNA. Perhaps, like me, my daughter would have her smile. Perhaps my son might inherit her big brown eyes, as my brother did. On the other hand, the idea of becoming a mother without my mother to guide me fills me with pain and fear. It is the thought that almost immediately brings tears to my eyes. And this is all before considering the other myriad reasons a person may or may not want children.

When I speak to young people who have lost someone, one of their most common regrets is that their parent, sibling or friend won't be able to give a speech at their wedding, or become a grandparent, aunt, uncle or godparent, or become a parent themselves. Grievers begin to understand that, instead of being moments of unadulterated happiness in our assumptive worlds, these maturational events and major life transitions will inevitably be undercut by a sense of sadness and loss. No matter how much the griever anticipates what it will feel like for their person to be absent during a transitional event, it is not possible to grieve in advance. Ruminating for years over how painful it might be to have children won't reduce the pain of my mother's absence if I ever choose to do so. 'Like children who can grieve only to the best of their abilities at whatever point they've reached in development, adults can only grieve to the extent of their accumulated, lived experience,' writes Hope Edelman in *The AfterGrief*. 'We can intellectually imagine these milestones. We might even engage in a type of anticipatory mourning when we envision the secondary losses yet to come. The existential nature of a significant one-time event can only be experienced in real time, when it occurs. That's how we encounter our old losses in new ways.'

Young grievers miss out on the support that the deceased may have given them as they take on adult roles, such as spouse or parent. For example, 'motherless mothering' is a well-researched example of how parental loss can impact the griever's own parenthood. For women, losing a mother is regarded as a key turning point, after which the daughter loses her guide or source of identification for womanhood.[1] If this loss happens before the daughter has had her own children, she loses an important source of support: maternal grandmothers have been shown to provide particularly beneficial practical and emotional support to new mothers.[2] One study found that it was not just grief at losing their mother that women coped with upon becoming parents; they also grieved the loss of support they would have had and the loss of knowledge about parenting their mothers held, and experienced a heightened sense of responsibility and death anxiety, worrying that their children would have to suffer grief, too.[3] As we will see, some of these experiences are not exclusive to daughters who have lost their mum.

It is not just getting married or having children that triggers old grief as fresh loss: it is any transition, including getting divorced, leaving employment or becoming a grandparent. 'Such lifespan events may contain both joy and sorrow, a bitter-sweet reminder of what is cherished and also of what was lost. To gaze around and see our friends and relatives participating in the kind of relationships we can't have, especially at times of transition, only pokes the fire more,' says Edelman. On top of this, when we lose an *older* relative in particular, we lose any model for growing up. This can hamper a young griever's ability to fully flesh out their adult sense of self, resulting in a sort of imposter syndrome where we don't feel mature enough to be handling the things adults do. 'When we lose a parent, older sibling or beloved grandparent,' Edelman says, 'we also miss out on the opportunity to be validated by that person as we mature. That's a powerful form of secondary loss. Taking decisive steps into becoming an adult can feel like role-play.'

Finally, we grieve not only for ourselves, but for what our person lost themselves: the experiences *they* never got, the memories they never made. As we will see, becoming a grandparent when your own parent never lived to be one can re-trigger grief, even many decades after their death. These recurrent echoes of loss, which last our entire lifespan, are what makes quarter-life grief so distinct from experiencing significant grief for the first time in later life. When you lose young, your entire adult existence is marked with the knowledge of loss, the emotional recurrence of it, while a friend the same age can go through every transitional event in their life without feeling that undercurrent of sorrow. This is also the reason it is so absurd that society imposes an expectation that we should be 'over' grief within the space of months or even a couple of years. The reality is that it will touch us over and over again as we age. As we will hear in this chapter, maturational events come with complex feelings of loss, happiness, gratitude, sadness and envy – a cocktail that those around us can fail to realise is happening. When we are bereaved young, the task of grief lasts a lifetime.

*

I met Alice Casely-Hayford when she reached out to me after reading a piece I wrote for the *Guardian*. At the time, she worked at *British Vogue* as digital editor. She had published her own powerful feature in the magazine about getting married wearing the wedding dress created by her late father, renowned designer Joe Casely-Hayford. Alice's wedding took place only a few short months after Joe's death from cancer, in January 2019, when he was 62 and Alice was 29. I was struck by the photographs accompanying the piece. They depicted an archetypally happy occasion, full of laughter and love. Knowing that the joyful bride captured in those images was also in the throes of fresh grief made them even more moving.

When I sit down to speak to her, Alice has just had her first child, Arthur, with her husband, Sean. The couple have moved to Islington, near where Alice grew up, just in time for their son's birth, and Alice is still on maternity leave from Net-a-Porter, where she now works as content director. Her love of fashion is the direct influence of her father, which also had a lasting impact on her brother's career, too. 'All our careers are very interlinked,' she says. 'We did everything as a family. My brother and my parents worked together. It meant that when he was diagnosed, there was a sense that, even though the cancer was advanced, we would all get through it together.' Alice's father founded his eponymous label with his wife, Maria, in 1984. The couple were partners, professionally and romantically, for the rest of Joe's life. Alice's brother, Charlie, worked for the business and still helms the Casely-Hayford label today. 'My father was my best friend and my mentor,' says Alice. 'My parents' relationship was really a fairy-tale and it was something I'd always wanted for myself. They were just the most archetypal, beautiful representation of love. That's the reason I am so grateful that my father got to meet Sean, who's my soulmate, even though he sadly didn't live to see me marry him.'

Alice was 26 and still living at home when the family were informed of Joe's diagnosis. 'I was an old young person to be still living at home, but I was so close to my parents, I was just not able to fly the nest!' laughs Alice. Her parents' relationship and their professional successes were something Alice grew up wishing to emulate, and she derived confidence from her father's support. 'My father was so careers-focused, but, at the same time, the number-one family man. He had the capacity to juggle both so perfectly. My beloved brother and I grew up in my parents' studios, but we never felt neglected or overshadowed by how passionate they were about their jobs. When I started working as a fashion journalist, my father was very encouraging and pushed me. He did it not in a "pushy parent" way, but in a way to make me believe so much in myself without any cockiness or arrogance. He was incredibly supportive.' Alice recalls how her father would leave positive comments under an alias on all her early blogposts and published articles. 'They'd say things like, "Oh my God, Alice, this piece is absolutely fantastic!"' she laughs. Alice inherited her father's passion and work ethic. 'I learnt some of my best qualities from him. We were such similar people that I feel like I've lost a huge part of myself.'

Alice's admiration of her parents' relationship meant that finding and marrying her 'other half' was high on the agenda from a young age. 'I was always excited to do it. I had a vision that I would have children at 22 because I was desperate for my parents to be around for as long as possible to help me raise my kids. My father loved children, which is why it's so devastating he won't meet mine. My parents were such an incredible influence on me that I wanted them to do the same for my kids.' When Alice's father was diagnosed, she was still 'desperately single'. 'In a selfish way,' she says, 'that was one of the biggest blows. I thought, *Oh, my dad's not going to be around for me to meet my soulmate and be at that next stage of my life.*' Thankfully, a few months later, Alice met Sean. Watching them build a relationship was something she felt very grateful for. 'Sean and

Dad had the most incredible relationship. They got the chance to get to know each other for three and a half years. I'm so grateful he got to meet my soulmate. Sean was able to ask my dad for my hand in marriage. That's very old-fashioned and traditional, but my dad was incredibly traditional, so I feel very privileged that happened.' When Sean proposed to Alice, they flew to Ghana – where her father was from – the same day. 'It was an amazing thing for Dad to see me discover more of my identity and see my sense of self and home grow through that trip and the engagement.'

Even though Sean and her father got on, Alice still felt the loss that Sean would not be able to spend more time with him. 'I felt very frustrated that my dad was sick by the time he and Sean met, because I feel that he wasn't maybe the best version of himself. He was suffering, and he was so brave in his suffering, but it wasn't my "true" dad, I guess, or it wasn't every part of my dad that Sean got to see.' Joe's illness meant that Alice and Sean's relationship was tested early on. 'It was a really strange time to be meeting the love of my life,' she says. 'You should be in this honeymoon period, which I was, but often after work I'd be running straight to the hospital. It was a big burden very early on in my relationship, how emotionally fraught and fragile I was with Sean. There were a lot of tears from day one. In a way it brought us closer because, to some extent, your partner has to see you at your lowest.'

Between her father's diagnosis when she was 26, and the time of his death when she was 29, Alice experienced many major changes: getting engaged, visiting Ghana, buying her first flat and landing her 'dream job' at *Vogue*. Though she was grateful that her father lived to see these milestone moments, she still feels that her grief – and the way it has changed her, ultimately – began when she was 26. 'There were so many milestones that he was a part of that I feel very grateful for. It was a whirlwind period. It's only now that I'm catching my breath. I didn't realise at the time, I was in the midst of a nervous breakdown by 2019, the year my dad died, because it was just this implosion of so many different things I'd taken in my stride without really confronting them.'

Joe's ill health prompted Alice and Sean to get married sooner, to maximise the chances of him being there. They set the date for March 2019. 'I'd always imagined I would get married in my early twenties, and I was fast approaching 30, so I thought, I've got to get married. I'm not someone who really dreamt about her wedding day, but I knew two truths: that my dad would walk me down the aisle, and that he would design my wedding dress.' However, Joe's health began to rapidly decline in December, four months before the wedding would take place. 'By Christmas, he was in a hospice. We were told he was only going there to "get better", which seems comical now, because who goes to a hospice to get better?' Realising they were running out of time, Alice and her father began the process of designing her dress. 'I knew that my dad walking me down the aisle was becoming increasingly less likely. I still thought he might be there, in a wheelchair or something. Really, really hurriedly, in the final stages of his life, we had to design this dress and then find someone who could help bring it to life.' Alice trusted her father to understand her style instinctively. She told him she wanted something 'a bit Grace Kelly', but he was underwhelmed by the idea and told Alice to think of something less obvious. In the end, he relented and sketched a modern take on the dress Kelly wore to marry the Prince of Monaco in 1956. The dress featured finger loops at the end of fitted sleeves, a silk cummerbund and a scallop-edged lace neck. 'He totally understood what I wanted, better than I'd understood [it] myself. I hoped he'd still get to see me wear it. It was painful that he died in January, which was so close yet so far from my wedding day.'

How did it feel when Alice put on the dress, on the morning of her wedding? 'Lots of people were like, "Oh, gosh, you can feel him here," on the day. I didn't necessarily feel that. But to have worn the dress he designed was a beautiful, beautiful thing. My darling brother – we couldn't be more different, but he is in a different way a manifestation of my father – he was able to walk me down the aisle and that was incredible, although incredibly tragic at the same time.' Despite her father's palpable absence, the rest of the day was 'perfect'. 'It was so full of love and joy and there wasn't a dry eye in the house. When he was in the hospice, my dad had helped my brother to write the father-of-the-bride speech, which my brother delivered in the voice of my dad and it was one of the most moving moments of my life. I don't feel he was there, but I know how happy he would have been. It was everything I wanted it to be, and he would only have approved of it.'

While getting married and having children are seen as moments of happiness and fulfilment, they are also transitions that can trouble our sense of identity. We leave one chapter behind while embracing another. For Alice, embracing life as a wife and then a mother led her further away from the version of herself her father had known and nurtured. 'In my early career, I was known as Joe's daughter because I was in the same industry as him. My name preceded me because my dad was so well known. I was so proud to be my dad's daughter and am still proud to be his daughter and to be a Casely-Hayford. It meant

I felt a loss of a sense of self after he died because I don't have that huge part of me [anymore]. Of course, I'm still his daughter, but in a way he's no longer my dad because he's no longer here.' Alice turned 30 a month after her wedding and left her job at *Vogue*. The changes were difficult without her father's guidance. 'I didn't feel like I knew who I was. It was really tricky. He didn't hold my hand through everything, but he was the person I'd go to before making any big decision, and now I'm such a different person to the person he was and that he made me.'

Although Alice always knew she wanted children, losing her father slowed the impulse. 'When I met Sean, we moved in together quite swiftly. It was quite frightening in a way because, when Dad was ill, I constantly felt I was holding onto something that was slipping away. Though finding out I was pregnant was an incredibly magical moment, there was also a sense of sorrow that my beautiful boy would never meet my beautiful dad. I don't think it's fully hit me yet because I'm still in a newborn bubble of happiness. My baby has my dad's eyebrows and he pulls certain expressions where he looks just like him. The Casely-Hayford gene is quite strong, so he looks very much like Dad.'

Forming her own family meant Alice felt distanced from the childhood with her parents she had so cherished. 'My son's last name is my husband's last name, so I feel like even less of a Casely-Hayford now. It's been a strange experience getting married and drifting further from that sense of self. The other day, I changed my homescreen on my phone to a picture of me, Sean and our baby. It had been a picture of me, my mum [and] my brother when we were little. Obviously, I couldn't be happier that I have such a wonderful family of my own, but it was like, *Wow, I've really closed that chapter*, and it really felt like that, which is devastating to me. I can't ever get that time back where I was so incredibly happy and it was so defining of who I am. I know a lot of new mothers experience that loss of identity, but mine is definitely exacerbated or compounded by the grief at moving away from the person my dad knew.'

I ask Alice about that sense of adulthood impostor syndrome; whether she, like me, feels a part of herself is fixed at 26 years old, still needing her father and feeling scared of life without him. 'Oh, totally! That's why I'm like, *How am I holding a baby? I'm still a teenager!* Time stopped when [Dad] was diagnosed but also accelerated so much,' she says. 'And because time has moved on and so much has changed, I can't always imagine what my dad's advice would be now. I know him inside out and when he was alive, I would have been able to predict what his advice would be, but now I really can't. Every day that passes, it feels like he's further away. After he died, I could remember all the conversations we had when he was in the hospice. Now, I have to recreate the reality of those in my mind. I want to tell those things to my son, but I feel I'm confusing and embellishing things, which is scary.'

Alice describes how grateful she feels that her husband is helping to actively cultivate a connection between her son and his late grandfather. 'Sean adored my dad and wants to keep his spirit alive. My dad will obviously not be as big of an influence on Arthur's life as he was on mine, but it's nevertheless important that he is very present. Sean is brilliant in that way. Dad and I shared a great interest in music, so I've already started to play Arthur his favourite songs. Dad also had a wicked sense of humour, which I inherited, so I hope to share that with Arthur, as well as Dad's morals and work ethic.' I wonder if Alice will be able to regain her own sense of identity through helping her son connect with her father. 'Becoming a parent has helped to bring me closer to him. He was an incredible parent. He saw himself as a father and a husband first and foremost. His job was important, but we were his greatest achievement. That's what I want to emulate, in my marriage and as a parent. That's what I hope will bring me closer to him again.'

*

Like so many young grievers I spoke to, Alice felt a dual sense of being frozen in time at the age she was touched by grief and an accelerated maturity. Part of that unsettled adult identity was driven by how frightening life felt without her father in it. As we have heard, the pervasive feeling of fear is incredibly common for mourners. For quarter-life grievers, death-oriented anxiety can become a driving force, feeding into every adult decision and maturational event that occurs. This was evident when I spoke to Josh, who lost his sister when he was 17. Now in his forties, Josh is married, has four children and works as a successful barrister. His profession is evident when he talks to me: he is careful and precise with his words, stopping in the middle of sentences to amend them so he can articulate exactly the point he is trying to make.

Josh embodies a very traditional image of success and aspiration. 'I live in a beautiful house with four gorgeous children and a lovely wife,' he says. 'But I spend a considerable amount of time each day worrying that one of my children might die today. When I stand back and think about it, it's amazing how many decisions and how many aspects of my life, large and small, I rearrange and calibrate and curate around the idea of imminent death. Every single milestone relates back to it in some way. It's just a permeating fact of my life. Death is an enormous presence in my world. I think about it literally all the time. I've got my own family now, but there's always, always that absence.'

Josh's older sister, Abigail, died when she was 22. Although she was born a healthy child, she developed cerebral palsy and epilepsy as a result of medical negligence. 'It was the mid-1970s. In those days, there was no support. My mother was 24. My parents were not well-off; they were training to be social workers. The doctors were very grandiose. They looked at the ceiling while they told my mother what had happened to her newborn baby. They handed my mother this child and sent her home with very little else. My parents had to figure out how to care for her on their own.'

Abigail required 24-hour care, with which Josh helped from a young age. Though the family received some support from charities and care nurses, they took on the majority of Abigail's care. 'We grew up as this happy, close family with some real difficulties. I had a very lovely relationship with Abigail – a caring relationship. It never occurred to me that she may have a shortened life expectancy.' But when Josh was preparing for his A levels, Abigail's health drastically declined. Josh's family were told she would not recover. 'The process of her decline – which was quite quick – was more traumatic than her actual death,' he says. 'When she died, it was calm, at home, in the living room, gentle. But the sudden decline where you panic – you get home from school, the front door is wide open, the house is full of people. It's very traumatic. If you think, *Where does grief begin?* It begins when the doctor tells your family she's dying. When I think of her death, I think of that moment, rather than the particular moment in February when she actually died.'

From the night that Abigail died, Josh tried to be a support to his parents, while feeling the incredible guilt of being the child left behind. 'I remember thinking to myself, *You must be strong, you must look after your parents*, and proceeding to do so even though they are incredibly strong people and would have wanted it the other way round. I can remember within hours saying to my mum, "We're going to be fine. She wasn't well. She will be remembered as young and not having to go through her illness into adulthood, which would have been awful. It would have been so hard to care for her when you got older. This is for the best; this is how it was meant to be." Lots of clichés, lots of truths. I remember having that conversation within three hours of her body being taken away. I felt a profundity of responsibility to make things OK for my parents. Then, of course, it lasts for the rest of your life because imagine letting your parents down when you're their only surviving child. Imagine wasting your life when you're the only one left.'

Josh felt a responsibility to reassure his parents that he was all right, even when he wasn't. 'I benefited greatly from having parents I could talk to,' Josh says. 'It's different to losing a parent because the two most supportive rocks in my life, my mum and my dad, are still here. But after a while – and it was sooner than I was expecting – they made it clear that they didn't want to talk about it every time we saw each other. They were both trained social workers, and incredibly emotionally literate, but they were trying to move on with their lives. It was incredibly traumatic to see both of them bereaved. I lived with that particular legacy my whole life and it's probably as profound as my own grief – the unbelievable guilt of being alive and the pressure it puts on me.'

After the funeral and returning to school, it became apparent that Josh couldn't expect any support from his friends or his teachers. 'I'm Jewish. You're probably aware that the funeral happens the day or two after the death, and then there's *shiva*, which is the prayers at home. It's very immediate, as it is with Islam. I can remember a very large group of my friends turning up to *shiva*. I found out, and it wasn't any great secret, that after this lots of them went out for dinner, then went back to one of their houses and did a combination of get drunk, smoke marijuana and watch pornography. To be perfectly blunt about it – it was 1998 and we were 17-year-old boys, that's the sort of thing many of them did on a Saturday night. I can't tell you how much that upset me when I found out. I struggle to articulate exactly why. I certainly don't rationally expect my friends to walk around in mourning because their 17-year-old friend's sister died. It was the sort of thing they were upset to hear. But did it impact on them? No, not really.

'My male friends at that age didn't have the capacity to be in any way supportive beyond the most basic sense for a couple of days,' Josh continues. 'I was perfectly willing to talk about things, as I am now, but that option wasn't there for me. One or two of them tried, but it was almost *my* generosity towards *them* that kind of closed down the conversation, because it was evidently so difficult for them. Funnily enough, a lot of them are my friends today and some of them will ask me about it, and now, as adults, with their own children, will show a much greater degree of emotional range. The world's changed as well. Men have changed. There was no real support at all at the time.'

With his parents unable to talk about Abigail's death, and no support from school or friends, Josh was left to handle his grief alone. 'I very much felt I had a long life ahead to deal with this, and what on earth is this going to look like in 10, 20, 30, 40 years' time? Because it's *never* going to go away. It's just an overwhelming feeling when you're young.' Josh had been planning to spend a gap year teaching English in India, but he cancelled the trip and went straight to university. He read English literature at Oxford. There, he immediately fell into a 'very intense' relationship with a girlfriend who became the focus of his world throughout his three years there. 'It was probably born out of wanting to hold onto a female relationship that wasn't my parents, but someone who was close to me,' he says.

Another factor contributing to the intensity of Josh's attachment was his increasing sense of anxiety. 'She had two brothers and a big family, and that was nice, to be part of someone else's family life. It might be as simple as describing it in its opposite: not sleeping alone. When I was alone, at university, I would find myself spontaneously just uncontrollably crying in my room or in my bed at night. It would always come back to that. Obviously, it would. It would come into my head suddenly at night, but in the daytime I wouldn't acknowledge it as an issue. My grief was incredibly fresh and, looking back, I was a very unhappy person at university. Now I think, *Wow, I can't remember a day at Oxford when I didn't have what would now be called acute anxiety*.' At the time, Josh passed his anxiety off as exam stress or homesickness. Though he is better able to recognise it now, it still affects him. 'I still very much feel when things go badly, I take it to high levels of catastrophising very quickly. I'm sure it's because I witnessed the ultimate things-going-wrong. For most people, the answer to catastrophising is to say, "Well, it probably won't happen." For me, I very much believe it will.'

The death-centric anxiety that stemmed from Abigail's death influenced Josh's adult life and decisions far beyond the first few years of his grief. In particular, it impacted his choices around children. 'Lots of people don't want children straight away,' he says, 'but when I got married to my wife, I was always very keen to have them quickly. There's something very fundamental to me about wanting to create new life and wanting to almost recreate a family that's been cut or cut short. Having four children is quite a lot – in fact, we had wanted five, but life got in the way.' Josh admits that part of wanting multiple children was mitigating the risk of any of them becoming an only child if their sibling died, as had happened to him. 'One can't escape odd thoughts like that,' he says. 'That's part of my obsession with death. I'm always planning my life around the next death waiting to happen.'

Despite Josh's eagerness to grow his family, having children amplified the fact of Abigail's absence. 'It brought back so much for me. My eldest daughter is 9 and she has my sister's name as her middle name. She looks a bit like her. She has the same colouring, the same hair, the same eyes. There's a physicality. One can overstate these things, but my parents almost saw her as filling a gap that had been left. They *adore* her. They *dote* on her, in a way I can't begin to – they've been great parents to me, but my God, not like that. They worship the ground she walks on. I suppose looking for replacements – looking for ways to balance the equation – is something you're constantly doing. Maybe it's what I was doing with my university girlfriend and the intensity of that relationship. Maybe it's what we are constantly doing throughout our lives. But I definitely feel there are moments of "re-grieving", and having children was one of those moments for me. I can never escape the fact that my wife and my children only know my sister from photographs. It constantly recreates the sense of trauma around her death.'

It is not only the fact that Abigail won't meet his children that has made having them difficult. The relationship between them as siblings reminds Josh of the bond he never got to enjoy. 'I feel a sense of loss constantly when I see what they have that I didn't,' he says. 'That's also to do with her having been so unwell and having such a compromised life. I never got the chance to play with her in the kind of vigorous or physical way that my children play together as brothers and sisters. It's not just my children, it's also when I see my wife's relationship with her sister. I often think, when my parents die, that's the end of my family. I now only have my new family. I hate that thought. When my wife's parents die, she still has a whole plank that's there in her generation. I know not everyone is close to their siblings, but when I look at other sibling relationships, I think, that's a real shame. I wish I could have had that.'

Josh's grief affects his parenting style, something he perceives clearly in comparison to his wife. 'She's never experienced grief in any significant way. She's 44 and she hasn't experienced it yet, so she just doesn't have the level of concern I feel about our children, or the worry I have over something happening to them, because, to her, these things don't happen every day. Whereas I see it happening every day, all the time. My wife worries about her parents dying. They're in their eighties, and it will be very sad when they do. But it has not informed her decisions about school, about university, getting married, having children, none of it, because she hasn't experienced it yet. When she does, it will be sad, but it will be with a whole life behind her and, in fact, probably only half or under half of her life remaining. For me, every adult decision I've made has been or will be informed by that loss.'

Sensing he has focused too much on the negative aspects of his anxiety, Josh adds that it has also fuelled him in more positive ways. 'It's important to say that some of it is positive,' he smiles. 'It's a driver, but it can be a driver of good things. I'm absolutely certain it's one of the reasons I've had the ethic to work hard and be successful. It's the need to live a life because you recognise the limits and pressures of time. No doubt about that. The presence of death is a very driving force as well as a limiting one. It haunts you in everything you do. There's a paradox, living with death at the heart of your life. But I find it easier to talk about things now. I don't feel any less sad, but as you get older, you find [that] a steeliness and a wisdom grow. I've found I've changed a lot in the last decade.'

Even though Josh has grieved Abigail's loss for many more years than he got to share with her, he finds it powerful that her memory is still palpable 25 years on. 'Last week, we had a big party in my garden for my parents' golden wedding anniversary. We had a big marquee, and it was a very beautiful, sunny day. Both mine and my father's speeches contained parts about my sister. My children heard those memories. A lot of my friends and their friends remember her. *So* many years down the line, so many people's minds were focused on it. So many people came up to me and said how much my sons and daughters looked like my sister. People see it because they want to see it. They want to tell you they haven't forgotten. That's comforting, because I haven't forgotten. It's something I will never forget.'

*

Quarter-life grief impacts your adulthood decisions, including whether and when you decide to undergo major maturational events. The way in which the young mourner's identity changes after adopting new roles, such as parent or spouse, can affect their relationship with the person they lost, as well as with the grief itself. This was true for Claire Cartwright, an actress and mother of two, who suffered the death of her father at 12, and her mother 10 years later, when she was 22. Claire talks about how her parents' absences are a key reason why she has never married the father of her children, and how becoming a mother changed her feelings towards her own father.

I met Claire at the same time I met Emily (see Chapter Three: First Love). The two were friends at university and Claire provided invaluable support to Emily when her mother died. Each had written me a letter, full of love, guidance and support, when they heard my letter being read out on *The High Low*. The first time I met Claire, she was pregnant with her first child. By the time I speak to her for this book, she has just discovered she is pregnant with her second. I meet her in Marylebone after an early scan, sometime after lockdown restrictions have been lifted, and we talk about how the pandemic – and recovering from it – is much like grief. Only when it's substantially in the past can you begin to process it and add a narrative to it.

Claire is expressive, funny and lively. She begins her story with the death of her father, who died from complications relating to alcoholism when Claire was 12. 'He was a complex figure,' she says. Claire's father and mother had had a very difficult relationship. She had older siblings who 'bore the brunt' of the fighting, shielding Claire in the process. When she was around six, her father moved back to Uganda, where he'd grown up. 'We'd never had a straightforward relationship. He went to Africa, which is *far* … I didn't see him much. In the same way when someone dies, when someone leaves and goes that far away, you're left to sort of make it up.'

Claire was left to imagine much of her relationship with her father. They kept in contact through letters, which her father would write in code. 'He would draw a deer for "Dear", and an éclair with the E crossed out for "Claire". I spent ages deciphering these letters. So it was quite a sort of romantic, long-distance relationship.' Claire's father was an alcoholic and was often ill. Despite this fact, his death still came out of the blue. 'He was always ill, always had malaria. I knew he had a problem with booze but, at 12, I didn't expect him to die. He died in Uganda of liver failure. Which was tricky. In many ways, he'd been so far away for a really long time, so it didn't change my day-to-day. When you lose someone you don't see all the time, but they're your dad – so on paper it's terrible – for a 12-year-old to get their head around what that feels like and what it actually means and what it does to your life … Does it change anything? Ultimately, not a lot. Not as much as your father dying *should*.'

Struggling to understand and adapt to her father's death, Claire grieved heavily for some years. 'I suddenly went off the rails at school and I couldn't really get my shit together. My mum was of the generation where she was quite stoic and she was amazing, but it was tricky for her to know how to communicate with me because Dad had been such a difficult figure in our lives.' A turning point came for Claire when she was 14, when she was able to foster a deeper and more spiritual connection with her father. 'Before, I had been super anti-Christian. I suddenly refused to sing hymns or say prayers in assembly and if you'd fucking told me to, I'd, like, give you one … *age 12*. I thought, if God's around, he sounds like a *dick*. But then somehow I was able to twist this experience from being over-whelmingly negative and bewildering to something positive. I felt I could communicate with him and I'd have conversations with him. If I was going into an exam and hadn't revised, I'd be like, *Help!* And somehow I'd smash the exam. And I'd think, *Possible explanation: my dad pulled some strings up there, wherever he is,*' she says, gesturing up at the sky. 'I had enough examples that it allowed me to believe and feel comforted by the belief that he was actually with me and listening to me.'

This new spiritual connection to her father allowed Claire to imagine him as a much more positive figure than he'd been when he was alive. 'I felt much closer to him and he was a much purer idea, purer being, than he had been in life. When I could make him up, he became this superhero who I really liked spending time with and who didn't let me down or leave me when I needed him. That was life-changing in a really good way. I felt supported in a way I never had. It was a hugely formative shift in my perception of things because I took responsibility for it, where before I'd looked to other people to be responsible for coping with my grief. I'm quite proud of it, looking back, because it's stood me in good stead. I've retained a lot of that spiritual sensation.'

As a young woman, before she had become a mother or lost her own, Claire enjoyed remembering only the positive version of her father. 'Because my dad was an alcoholic, and deeply charming and wild, and the life and soul of a party, and attractive and charismatic, and the person everybody wanted to be with and have a conversation with, he's remembered by his friends as this super-turbo-hero. My brother has some of that; he really idolised him. I was fed these wild stories of my dad, like [him] walking home from a party barefoot at 5 a.m. because

Mum had left him because he was being a dick, or the night I was born, he threw a huge party while Mum was in the hospital. There were endless stories of his wildness and, as a teenager, they chimed with what I thought was important and fun. I read books and watched films where the heroes were like wild, untameable beasts. I thought my dad was *that* cool.'

Did that lead to her emulating him? 'I mean, I'm a party girl,' she says bluntly. 'I love a good time, I respect people who can throw a good party. I don't have an "off" button. But I don't have an addictive personality. So, while I can be the last one at a party, and I might feel like shit the next day, I don't keep drinking. My father did; he kept going. So there was a bit of emulation, but thankfully not a complete one.'

Claire's relationship with her father, and the almost mythical regard in which she held him, were both altered when she lost her mother. 'Mum was diagnosed with cancer when I went to university and almost as soon as she got engaged to my stepfather, who was the best thing that had happened to her. They'd been together for some time, but their engagement was … it was their time, you know? After all the difficult years with no money and three children to look after on your own because their father is some goon who can't do anything to control himself … that was a real tragedy.' Claire had to go through the brutal process of watching her mother deteriorate over two years. She died just as Claire was preparing for her finals.

Claire had assumed she would be hit with the same wave of grief as she had been as a 12-year-old on learning her father had died. But the experience was completely different, because her relationship with her mother was fundamentally different. 'She had always been everything. She was the opposite of my dad, who'd been this kind of absent non-parent. She'd been two parents and done an unbelievable job. She was – in the same way as yours was – my absolute universe.' Claire tried to prepare herself and those around her for her mother's death. 'I remember saying to all my uni friends, "Yeah, get ready, 'cause I'm about to lose my shit."' She acts the conversation back and forth. 'They were like, "OK, OK." They asked, "What's it gonna look like?" and I said, "You'll know when you see it." And then it happened and everyone was waiting, but I had to do my finals, so I said, "OK, after finals, I'm going to fall apart." Then I went straight to drama school, and it was like, "Any minute, guys, I'm gonna lose it." But then I'd have to do auditions, so it was, "After these auditions, I'm gonna really lose it." They were all prepared for it. But it never came. I didn't have time to come off the rails like I had with Dad, because I just had to deal with it and live my life.'

After her mother's death, her father faded as the parent occupying that spiritual space in Claire's brain. 'Mum replaced the relationship I'd had with Dad in the stratosphere, because of *course* she did. I still have a semblance of him being there, but he's not who I ask for things or ask for advice.' When she became a mother herself, she reassessed her father and his actions altogether. 'How I felt about him shifted partly when Mum died, but partly because I'm a mother myself. Now, I think, *What a dick!* My whole relationship with the stories his friends would tell, and the creation I'd been part of and complicit in, the way I'd tell them proudly at parties to my friends ... Having children has smashed a lot of that scaffolding I had erected as a young person to hold him up as this mythical figure. I suddenly had a mother's perspective. My partner is unbelievable. He's the kindest, most thoughtful, generous, amazing dude, and I've gone through parenthood with someone like that, and I've just thought, *Fuuuuck you* towards my dad. *Fuck you for being so shit.*'

These new thoughts Claire experienced were difficult, especially as she wasn't able to confront her father about them. 'It was a feeling I'd never had before,' she says. 'I suddenly found an anger where it hadn't been before, about his life and the way he behaved when he was alive. My relationship with him has changed in a – "ugly" isn't a nice word, but in a challenging, not-positive way. And the problem is, you can't talk it out. There are things I'd like to put to my dad. There are questions I'd like answered. And it's not possible. It's hard to work through. For a conversation, you need that other side, you need the response. When it's just a one-sided conversation, there's nowhere for those feelings to go.'

Claire had always known she would have children but, to date, she has avoided getting married. 'I sort of couldn't bear it,' she says. 'My partner's family are really … *alive.*' Intact? I offer. 'Yes. A mum and a dad, still married, alive. He's got a sister, too. And I just couldn't face it. I've been to so many weddings, because I'm in that time of life. They are such a lovely thing. I'd love to do it. But I think I'd cry all day. I hope I will do it one day, but I sort of decided that me having my own children and my own family would lessen … the *spice* of that grief, of getting married and having neither parent anywhere. I just couldn't fucking do it.'

Claire always knew having children would be difficult, more so than any other big milestone. 'The first time I performed in the West End, I cried all night,' she says. 'Every time anything good happens – and the better it is, the harder it is. First big job, first anything, it's brutal, but you …' 'You can find other people to celebrate with?' I ask. 'Yes. But having children is so family-oriented. You so want to share it. I always knew it would be the biggie because, on her deathbed, I had this amazing conversation with Mum.' Claire was prompted to talk to her mother by the palliative care nurse. 'She was called Jill. I was in the kitchen with her, cooking, having a shit time. Jill said, "Have you told your mum you love her? Because there's not going to be long left." And I was like, "Yeah." And she said, "But have you had the conversation *now*, in this moment?"'

Claire was scared to have this talk. 'Mum was deeply unemotional; she wasn't someone that would ever sit there and go, *I love yooou*,' she says, putting on a sad soap-opera accent. 'So I didn't know how she was going to take it. I went into her room and she was having quite a calm moment. And I said to her – I really kind of looked into her eyes, and I told her I loved her. And we had this amazing conversation, which has stayed with me forever, and I will remember so vividly forever, and I'm so grateful that I did it and so grateful Jill told me to do it. I said, "I love you," and she burst into tears and I burst into tears.' Claire pauses and I can see her eyes are turning red. I can feel the sting of tears in my eyes, too. 'And then she gave me the biggest smile and she said, "We've had fun, haven't we?" And I was like, "Yeah, we've had *such* a good time." It was so … It was the perfect thing to say because we'd had such fun together. It was amazing and then – sorry—' Claire starts to cry and I tell her not to be sorry, because I am crying, too. She takes a breath. 'And then she got a bit upset because she was like … "The worst thing is, I won't ever see you get married and have your children." So those things were always going to be— She didn't need to say it for me to know that, but it does slightly ring in my ears anyway. They were always going to be the *real* spicy bits. It's a bugger. It is a bugger.'

The sense of loss is heightened when Claire sees friends whose parents have become grandparents. 'It's brutal. It's absolutely brutal. Obviously, one should never compare and we're all lucky in our own way, etc. But, Christ, some people are *so* lucky. It gives you another opportunity, one that's hard to resist, to look round and be like, *Well, it didn't work out for me that way*. It reignites the unfairness that goes through your head sometimes when you're grieving. I've got no one and haven't had for ages, and you've got all [your family] and you've had them this *whole time*. There's been no point where you haven't had them. They've been there the *entire time*. It reminds you of quite how long your parents have been gone. Having children is amazing, but it's the biggest emotional endeavour because you have to keep re-facing your grief, re-looking at it, re-examining it. You have a wonderful new presence, but it reminds you of the absence, and what you and they have lost.'

After her mother's death, her stepfather bought the house she grew up in. He has since found a new partner, but still welcomes Claire and her siblings there. It's allowed Claire to feel that her daughter can meet her grandmother, in some way. 'It's amazing because I've still got my bedroom from when I was a baby. I can take my daughter to my mum's grave and have my daughter in spaces my mum had been in. There's some energetic connection I can piece together through that. Robin, my daughter, will touch something that was my mum's, that my mum touched.' Like Josh, Claire can see elements of her mother in her children. 'If you're lucky enough to get pregnant naturally with your own genetics, that child is part of that person, and that's so nice. When I was pregnant the first time,

I remember thinking, *I'm quite literally putting a genetic bit of Mum back into the world*. You're creating a bit of the person you loved more than anything. I see flashes of her in my daughter's face all the time and bits of her personality. It feels a bit magical that you can recover bits of someone who was so completely lost to the world. But I still wish it was something my mother could have enjoyed. Because it's *beautiful*.'

*

This book has sought to show how grief interacts with all the rites of passage that might punctuate a young person's journey to adulthood. Getting married and having children are some of the 'biggies': the moments when we are seen as truly adult, whether we feel it on the inside or not. But grief doesn't end with these 'young' milestones; it continues to impact and influence upon 'older' milestones, too. To show us how, it is time to meet our final young griever. Her name is Kris and she is a grandmother. Now in her sixties, Kris lost her mother over 35 years ago, just after she had welcomed her second child. At the time, Kris worked in America and had to fly back to England with her husband to see her mother before she died. 'With a baby and a 19-month-old toddler, that was some feat,' she said.

Kris's mother had not yet met her grandson, who was only two months old. 'She was at home, in bed, and I was feeding the baby. After I fed him, I lay him on the bed. He was perfectly safe; he couldn't roll over or anything. She'd hardly looked at him the whole time. She wasn't interested in him and wouldn't engage with him. I thought, *I'll just leave him here*, and I went downstairs with the toddler to make a meal in the hope that my mother might engage with the baby. When I came back, I just found them both asleep. I don't think she could bear it. She couldn't bear the fact that she wasn't going to see him grow up.'

After her mother died, Kris returned to America with her husband. Her grief got 'completely lost' in the demands of young family life, though she still yearned for her mother's help. 'You have friends with small babies and you see them handing them over to their mothers. That's quite hard.' It was only when her own daughter reached the same age Kris had been when she lost her mother that she began to think about her grief. 'You look back and, at the time, you think you're an adult, but actually I was still very childlike in many ways. When my daughter reached the same age I just thought, *Gosh, how on earth did I cope?* I'd spent a long time wondering how I could have dealt with my mother's death better – how I could have helped her to engage with my son, or talked to her about the fact that she was about to die. But I couldn't have known; I was still so young. I've got 30 years' more experience now, including losing her, and the growth I've had through losing her.'

Kris re-examined her mother's loss further when her own daughter fell pregnant and had her first child. The baby boy arrived during lockdown. Her daughter had experienced a difficult birth from which it took a long time to recover. 'When I went round to stay with them a few weeks later, after isolating, I hardly thought about the baby. I was completely anxious and worried about my daughter. That really took me by surprise. Seeing her struggle, because she'd been quite badly physically affected by the birth, was hard. The baby never slept so my daughter was always very tired. I was more worried about my daughter, and I thought, *Golly, what's wrong with me? There's this lovely baby and I've hardly thought about him*. It was only when my daughter started to improve that I was able to engage with him more through practical things like taking him out for a walk so my daughter could get some sleep.'

Realising that her daughter was still her priority when her grandchild arrived, Kris was able to re-contextualise her mother's reaction to her newborn grandson. 'When my daughter's baby arrived, I thought, *Well, I don't need a baby, I've got a baby – my daughter's my baby. I don't need this other one to worry about,'* she laughs. 'It really took me by surprise. I'd not expected that at all. So for my mum, she was probably more worried about me when she was ill than she was about seeing my baby son. That's probably why she didn't engage with him. For me now, I'm completely besotted by my grandson and I help my daughter a lot. There are times where I've got up at half-past six every day in order to take care of him. No one else does that. My husband would never do that. None of my son-in-law's family do that. But the baby's mother is my daughter, and as her mother, I am motivated to get up early to look after the baby in order to look after her.' Knowing how strong her instinct was to mother her daughter in the early days of new parenthood, Kris suddenly realised how much she had lost when her own mother died. 'I never had anybody. I realised what I'd missed. Obviously, my husband and I looked after each other, but it was all a negotiation because we each needed looking after. The thing about a mother is, it's unconditional. You just do it because you're motivated. I'd rather not get up at half-past six in the morning, but I did want my daughter to get some sleep.' Bonding with her grandchild, Kris also felt sadness that her mother had never got to experience what it was like to be a grandmother.

A couple of years after Kris welcomed her first grandchild, she reached the age her mother had been when she died. 'If I went to a grief counsellor now, I think I'd be told that I hadn't properly grieved my mother until my daughter had her child. But what really cemented it was reaching 60, because that was the age when she was diagnosed, and she died a couple of months later.' A few months before Kris's sixtieth birthday, she herself was diagnosed with early-stage breast cancer. 'It was very early so I had a small operation and some radiotherapy, and I didn't need anything worse than that. But that brought a lot back for me.'

As she's begun to live through her sixties, Kris has found herself feeling as though she is facing a void. 'I'm 63 now, so I'm three years older; I've had three years that my mother never saw. That feels really strange, because I've got no template. I can't imagine what old age will be like. I now look very like my mum when she was 60, but I have no idea how she'd have looked at 80 or how her health would have been. How would she have coped with becoming less mobile, or becoming ill? When I look ahead, I can't imagine the future.' Faced with the unknown, Kris is put off from taking the next big transitional step and retiring. 'My husband's retired, but for me I find the idea very difficult. I've gone down to four days a week and with my one day off, my mission is to figure out what I'd like to do when I retire. It's the one time in my life I've felt I really don't know what's going to happen next.'

Despite this, Kris describes how her familiarity with grief has helped her to help others experiencing it. 'My daughter's sister-in-law had a brain tumour. She lived for a long time with it, but it spread and the end came very quickly. She was far too young to die. I don't think I could have helped my daughter or been as much support for my daughter if I hadn't experienced grief myself. I feel very proactive in trying to help her and help my son-in-law.' What has Kris learnt over 30 years? 'We had a lot to learn about grieving 30 years ago. It's amazing how things have come on. I think the thing I've learnt is that you have to do it. You really have to grieve, and it takes a long time. It's taken me 30 years to do it. You don't have to just carry on, you can take the time you need. You have to do grief in your own way.'

Seven

Future Grief

Digital afterlives, next-gen funerals and how our ways of grieving are changing

When I'm asked why I started The Grief Network, the simple answer is: because I couldn't find anything else like it. The more complex and more honest answer is that The Grief Network was an angry response to the question: *Why?* Why, in 2018, had no one figured out that young people might need their own tailored support? Why was I being left to deal with this alone? It doesn't take a psychologist to realise that this anger was partially misdirected: I was angry that the grief support I wanted didn't exist because I was angry that my mother had died in the first place. Why did she have to die? Why couldn't she survive a third time? Hadn't two cancers been enough? Why was I the one who had to lose her mum? It wasn't fair. I wanted more time. The problem was, I could never (and still cannot) think of the phrase *It's not fair* without hearing my mother's voice responding, *Life's not fair*. It was a phrase that punctuated my childhood, every time my brother or I would protest at not being given a chocolate bar or not being taken to the park or not being allowed to stay up to watch TV. 'It's not fair!' we'd cry. '*Life's* not fair,' she would say, somewhere between a quip and an admonishment. It stuck in my mind because it felt like an irrefutable, irrebuttable adult's truth. My child's brain could never find a way around it.

It's not fair, I thought over and over when my mother died. When I heard her voice responding, though, it was kinder now. *Life's not fair. People die.* She'd seemed to accept her death when she was ill. For me to accept it with grace, too, was to honour her. *Life's not fair* was, to an extent, comforting. It was the soft answer to the question: *Why her? Why me?* Well, people die. One of them happened to be your mum. But at the same time, *Life's not fair* was the shuttered storefront I came up against every time I fumbled my way towards feeling the rage I'd been told was inherent to grief. Like my father, I'd always had a quick temper, so I was baffled why I never seemed to feel any anger at my mother's death. I couldn't express it in a straightforward way because anger, we're told, is destructive, ugly, unkind. It's particularly indecorous for young women. And anyway, who would I direct that anger towards? It wasn't anyone's fault. If I couldn't be straightforwardly angry that it wasn't fair that my mum had died, I needed somewhere else to channel the feeling. The Grief Network was it.

This was the reason I struggled when friends or colleagues would tell me I was doing an amazing thing. They seemed to assume I was doing it out of the goodness of my heart. That wasn't true. As far as I was concerned, The Grief Network addressed my own selfish need to find other people going through the same thing, and to find the community I needed to process my grief. That sociality changed the landscape of those early years of grief, which would have otherwise continued to be achingly lonely. It also gave me a valid place to stand in public and shout about how fucking awful it was that Mum was dead, without admitting it was me, Rachel, feeling that rage. As the voice of The Grief Network, I could express how I felt on behalf of a group of overlooked people and be affirmed. If that helped others in the process, then great. Helping other young people and giving them a space to gather felt valuable and warm, but it wasn't the fire driving me. Pouring anger into the question *why isn't there support for young people?* was constructive. That was a question that had an answer, and it had a solution. It was a question I could do something about. It was a better question than *why is she dead?* which had no answer beyond the sad, limp fact of a cancer diagnosis. That was a permanently open-ended question, leading to open-ended pain, with no satisfactory answer.

I didn't know any of this, of course, at the time. It is something I have worked out in the five years of running the Network and hearing other young people talk about why they started similar initiatives. Seeing how the 'young grief space' has changed helped transform my view of grief from something that is purely personal, to something that also has the capacity to be social, cultural and political, and anger is a key part of why a change in grief support is happening. At the time of writing in 2023, the landscape of young grief support has changed drastically from what it was in 2018 when I set up The Grief Network. At that time, when I set up an Instagram account for the Network, the only other grief pages I found were abandoned blogs people had posted twice on and forgotten, or the odd account featuring strange morbid art. When I typed 'grief' into my podcast app, I thought to myself, *There must be a podcast about this by now*. There was one: Cariad Lloyd's brilliant *Griefcast*. That was it. Now, there are myriad podcasts, Instagram pages, apps, articles, and even 'grief influencers' to follow and interact with. It is a whole online environment many people refer to as the 'online grief community'.* There are more support groups for young grievers, some now established as small charities, though still not on a scale that makes them accessible to young people throughout the country.

What has driven this change? At the beginning, I thought it was down to the younger generation: Millennials, and now Gen Z. Millennials were the original snowflakes (a word I first heard used to describe how touchy-feely young people had got, long before it became a polarising political slur). We talked (or complained, depending on who you asked) about our mental health, which was poor because of the financial and political pressures we grew up with. Though grief hadn't been included in the conversation around mental health in 2018 as far as I could tell, I knew it was an optimal moment for it to begin to feature. I saw the emerging movement of young people talking about grief as a natural response from a generation unwilling to replicate our parents' stiff upper lip and suffer in silence.

Then the pandemic happened. As it was reported that, alongside immunocompromised people, those in older and middle age were most vulnerable to the coronavirus, I realised that if people in their fifties and sixties were dying in high numbers,

* Whether it is truly a 'community' or something that exists only 'online' is a topic we will come on to in this chapter.

they were probably leaving behind a lot of teenaged and twenty-something children. Inevitably, the number of followers on our Instagram account grew grimly, and every day we seemed to get follow requests from other accounts with 'grief' somewhere in the title. It was no longer a sad club of the few, but a predicament of the many, and there was a feeling that online grief support was a crucial lifeline for those who had been bereaved during lockdown. Unable to see friends or family, or hold a normal funeral, people turned to the internet to express their grief and find comfort and community. I was deeply saddened that we were unable to hold meet-ups; I knew the power of other people's presence to make you feel less alone. If grief in Western culture had already become a lonely and isolated thing, the lockdown restrictions made it even more so.

In Chapter One: Quarter-life Grief, we learned how the major transitions of the early twentieth century altered our grief culture drastically. The combination of the World Wars, the Spanish flu pandemic, social movements and advanced medical technology all contributed to the individualisation and abnormalisation of death and grief. As Hope Edelman notes, 'The dominant attitudes toward death, dying and bereavement that surround us today have more in common with the attitudes of 1920 than the attitudes of 1920 had with those that existed in 1910.' In 2023, we find ourselves in a similar landscape to a century ago. There is war in Europe in the aftermath of a global pandemic, with heated debates over identity politics and far-right ideologies re-emerging, in a hyper-connected world with technology developing at hyper-speed. These macro-trends are all having an impact on the way modern mourners grieve. Will new technology help or hinder the grieving process, as mourners are able to express their feelings on social media or even interact with the digital legacy of the dead? How do we address the diverse needs of all identities of grievers? And how do we renormalise grief if we cannot accept death? Will we change the way we mourn altogether?

*

New forms of media, made possible by the internet, are the obvious place to start. When I think of my own story, the unique part is not that I lost my mother when I was 26. It's that, in 2018, I had well-developed channels through which I could connect with other young people, in a way that a 26-year-old 10 years earlier would not have been able to. There was no Instagram in 2008. There were blogs and forums, but these did not exist in 'networks' that allowed users to broadcast themselves, and they were not advertised to users with the same power and specificity made possible by modern algorithms. (Follow one grief account on Instagram or TikTok now, and you will be offered a platter of similar accounts.) The word 'podcast' only entered the dictionary in 2006, having been coined in a *Guardian* article in 2004 and reaching mass popularity in 2014 when the radio programme *This American Life* launched the phenomenon that was *Serial*.[1] In the UK, in 2018, an estimated 11 million people per year listened to podcasts, rising to 21.2 million in 2022.[2]

The *High Low* podcast I wrote to was both wildly popular (downloaded 30 million times)[3] and semi-niche; I knew the listenership comprised other young women. At the same time, I had an intuitive understanding of how to use Instagram to build a 'brand', because I had seen small brands and businesses do the same as the platform became more widely used than the vintage photo effects app it once had been. The internet, and the new media it offered, had made it easier to find the specific individuals for whom a support group for young, bereaved people might be relevant. In 2023, the ability to advertise to a niche demographic has become even more powerful, with apps like TikTok's algorithms famously (and eerily) target specific.

On Instagram, I saw a proliferation of pages relating to grief. Though The Grief Network was very much intended to be an 'IRL' (in real life) initiative, using social media was the primary means by which we could communicate with members to let them know when the next event or meet-up would take place. In time, I saw personal blog pages turn into meme pages and subsequently into podcasts. Others began life as pages for illustrations or for sharing stories and evolved into event series. Some became full-blown grief influencers, accumulating tens of thousands of followers and creating daily posts about the realities of grief. This was the 'online grief community'. But what exactly is that, and what are people doing when they 'grieve' on social media? This is the question that Anna Geatrell attempted to answer through her (unpublished) research during her master's in anthropology at the University of Oxford. Immersing herself in the world of 'grief Instagrammers',* she studied the motivations of people who used social media to express their grief. She came to the conclusion, she told me,

---

* I use the term 'Instagrammers' as Geatrell's research focused on those using that platform. However, I believe her work is likely applicable to those engaging with other forms of social media, such as the emerging 'GriefTok' space on TikTok. Geatrell's thesis focused only on individuals creating content on dedicated grief accounts, rather than those who consumed or engaged with it.

that grief Instagrammers were 'emoting, participating, keeping quiet and hearing new callings'.

In emoting online, grief Instagrammers were using the platform to express their grief through creative means. The platform gave them the space to write, draw or share other content relating to their experience. It gave them an opportunity to express emotions where they perhaps had no other outlet. What was interesting, Geatrell said, was that this 'emoting' challenged the typical Western model of emotions. 'We think of emotions as static, so the process of posting about it online would be: *I have an emotion and I present it to you*. What I found grief Instagrammers were doing was understanding what their emotions were *through* the process of emoting online, so it was actually: *I present something to you and then I understand what I'm feeling*. It was through expressing it that they actually came to realise what their emotions were.' In that way, grief online was an active task, rather than a passive one, meaning they could participate. 'Participating is political, with a small P. In emoting in a public space, they are putting something on view that we are told we're not supposed to. That's a political act, because it's disruptive. It goes against expected behaviours.' Where Instagram has often been seen as a space for highlight reels or promotion (i.e. *good vibes only*), posting something 'negative' such as grief disrupted what was normally seen on a social media feed. 'Some of my interviewees actually described themselves as activist, with a small A, because they saw themselves as doing something that went against the norm.'

But grief Instagrammers were in constant negotiation between publicly emoting and participating, and choosing when to keep quiet. 'There wasn't a big difference between the online and offline "self",' said Geatrell, 'but there was a navigation of what to put out publicly and when to keep things to themselves. Deciding when to keep quiet, to keep something private, was an important part of finding out how they were feeling. One of my interviewees described it as a negotiation between the "punk rock" of being an online grief activist and then actually finding time to sit with their own grief.' This reminds me of one grief content creator I know who admitted that the person they lost was an addict, who could be unreliable and contributed to many unhappy childhood memories. That fact was not public, and neither were the more complex emotions of grief relating to it.

Finally, Geatrell found that grief Instagrammers were 'hearing new callings'. Where their pages had started out as a typical Instagram account, the activity often evolved into something else. 'This is interesting because it showed that, whatever people were doing online with their grief, it led them to doing something else. Some have started podcasts [or] charities, others have become death doulas. You are writing your book. That demonstrated that "grieving online" was not really to do with being online or being on Instagram at all.' Grieving online was one limb or expression of the entire task of grief, and online activities were part and parcel of processing grief. 'It's not just a single outpouring of emotion that is this one static thing called "grief",' she explained. 'It's actually an ongoing and strategic task, which is probably not separate to the task of grieving itself.'

Geatrell's findings resonated with my own brief experience of existing within the online grief space. There was something satisfyingly disruptive in posting about grief, with all its miseries and contradictions, and knowing that this wasn't really what was expected on social media at a time when the flawless lives of influencers still reigned. Geatrell described grief Instagrammers as doing something at the confluence of the 'therapeutic and creative'. Posting as The Grief Network allowed me to talk in a voice that was sardonic and realistic, but it also allowed me to reject the image of grief – and grief support – I'd received over 25 years by creating my own. I thought grief support was sitting in a town hall or church crypt with weak tea and Jammie Dodgers, uncomfortable or sobbing, when I'd probably rather be somewhere 'normal', like the pub. I had grown up at the dawn of best-friend brands: the chatty, bright and now-ubiquitous design that featured in start-up companies like Uber, Deliveroo, Monzo, Bumble and Netflix before they were household names. Going on bereavement charity websites and seeing photos of old people holding hands, the words 'we will guide you through your loss' plastered over it, massively put me off. I didn't want what my life looked like to change just because my mum had died. I still wanted to be young and occupy young spaces. Grief support groups weren't it.

Fortunately, two regular Grief Network attendees, Katy and Fiona, were brilliant graphic designers. They mocked up a logo and social media assets that took their cues from young, cool brands. We very consciously rejected the idea that grief should be dark and sombre. People commented positively on it: the look and voice of The Grief Network made those coming feel like it was more normal, or something they'd like to be a part of. One non-bereaved friend who attended an event once told me (somewhat sheepishly, knowing she wouldn't want to join the dreaded club herself) that she'd felt a slight pang of jealousy. Everyone there was so 'cool', and it was a great way to make friends and meet people our age. She didn't have any big club like that to go to herself. That was great to hear. It meant we were doing something right: making grief something that wasn't sad or shameful, something to hide or keep hushed. We were making support that people wanted to be involved in. Something that was creative and ... kind of cool. Eyes may roll. And to be clear, I am not saying grief needs to be made cool. I am saying that support should reflect the lives and needs of those it caters to. For young people, who are saturated in visual culture, from fashion, music and social media, what something looks like is important. Gen Z, for example, are 1.5 times more likely to follow a brand that provides content that boosts their own image.[4] Carving out a space online can also be a creative method by which young people can express themselves in a language that is natural to them – one which other young people will understand. Grief is not something that many will ever feel proud of, but making grief support accessible means making it something young people aren't ashamed to need or engage with.

New forms of media are allowing the bereaved to connect and express themselves in new and creative ways. Beyond young grievers, social media can be used as a tool to connect all kinds of grievers with different experiences. But the picture is not an entirely positive one, enabling straightforward connection, creativity and communication. The resources are not evenly distributed, for a start. Those in rural areas, or those from so-called 'hard-to-reach' communities, may be less likely to engage with grassroots initiatives housed or advertised digitally. When I ask Julia Samuel, somewhat hopefully, about the exponential growth of the 'online grief space', she is ambivalent, reminding me of the echo-chamber nature of social media. 'The jury is out on whether the benefits of social media outweigh the negatives,' she says. 'It is the people who don't look for help in the first place who are the most in danger of negative outcomes. If you're looking for support online, you're potentially not the person who needs help the most.' The UK Bereavement Commission (for which Samuel was a commissioner) found that over 40 per cent of bereaved people wanted formal help but did not get it.[5] Thirty-three per cent of respondents who wanted to access bereavement services indicated no support was available, while 37 per cent said they didn't know how to access support.[6]

Social media is also notoriously not designed to promote positive emotions, but to trigger negative ones. This leads to questions as to whether resources and initiatives intended to support vulnerable people are really best housed on digital platforms like Instagram. Indeed, many psychologists have expressed concerns at the rise of 'mental health influencers',[7] or therapy Instagram accounts, which offer advice but are no substitute for those formal resources. From speaking to some grief content creators I know, they reported often feeling either exhausted by the demands of creating content and interactions with their followers, or feeling excluded from the space altogether – something I could relate to. I asked Anna Geatrell about the labour that went into grieving online. Though her research did not address that specific question, she pointed to the many studies that highlight the strained relationship between content creation on digital platforms, labour and 'career'. Geatrell's research also suggested that the idea of the 'online grief community' was not entirely accurate. 'The closest term I would have used for it is a "coherent digital network", which sounds overly academic,' she laughs. 'But it's a network in the sense that the people using Instagram to talk about grief are connected. It's digital because it's housed digitally, and it's coherent in the sense that the topic is the same. That doesn't mean you can jump to the assumption that "community" suggests that people are harmonious.'

This point comes into focus when thinking about diversity. During the pandemic, when many were already very much online, the world was rocked by the news of George Floyd's murder by a police officer in Minneapolis, Minnesota. As Black Lives Matter protests swept the States and the UK, conversations began to take place about the 'whiteness' of the grief space online. Black and brown grievers reported how the cultural and racial challenges they faced in grief were not always welcome topics in grief support groups, or at least not readily understood by their white counterparts. This was true for Georgia Wickremeratne, who is Sri Lankan and Jamaican, and is one of six young women who run the Instagram page 'Grief Safe Space' for Black and brown grievers. She found that the 'racial undertones' in her grief were not something she felt able to discuss in predominantly white support groups. Georgia's biological father was Jamaican. Her stepfather, like the rest of her family, including two half-siblings, were Sri Lankan. He had raised Georgia since she was six years old. 'I never really felt any kind of way about that until he died,' she told me. 'When he was ill in the hospital with pancreatic cancer, a nurse came in and she only spoke to my brother and sister about him. I realised, *Oh my God, she doesn't even think I could be his child.*' This sense of difference, which Georgia had never felt while her stepfather was alive, was exacerbated when the wider family sent condolences to Georgia's mother and half-siblings alone. Feeling disenfranchised in her grief, Georgia resorted to finding support online. Speaking to other grievers of colour helped her to articulate what she was feeling. 'It allowed me to understand how much race can tie into something like grief. The Grief Safe Space is for everyone, but the stories we share are Black and brown. So much about culture and race tie into grief because in Asian or Black cultures, for example, talking about feelings is not something that is as fluid. There's a lot of shame. People of my generation are so grateful for an online space because they can't talk to their parents, because their parents process and handle things really differently.' Specific spaces for young grievers and grievers of colour are the things Georgia feels have been missing from traditional support.

Jermaine Omoregie lost his father in 2014 and his mother a year later in 2015, when Jermaine was still only in his early twenties. He hosts the *Thinking Out Loud* podcast with Ben Acquaah, who lost both his parents as a teenager. As part of the African diaspora, Jermaine and Ben regularly explore the cultural nuances that arise in grief and have discussed the pressure young men can feel to become the 'man of the house' in the face of loss. The podcast has focused on a wide range of topics, from baby loss, sibling loss and suicide, to issues of funeral debt, fatherless fathering and what it's like to come from a so-called 'broken home'. Jermaine and Ben stand out within the grief space not only for their race, but for their gender, something of which Jermaine is aware. 'There are definitely more women in the space,' he says. 'As a Black man, if I can be an example, other guys can see me talking about things and can think that they can also talk about these things and know they're not alone.' I ask him whether he ever felt the pressure not to talk about his grief for fear of not being seen as masculine. 'Masculinity is something that changes so much. I've always been someone who really wears his heart on his sleeve. A lot of times, guys are suffering in silence. They bottle it up maybe out of ego or maybe because they haven't got anyone in their close circle they can talk to. Everyone's different, but for me it's about speaking from the heart. My mental health is more important than my masculinity.'

Not everyone's experience of talking about diversity in grief has been as positive. Callsuma Ali set up the brilliant *Bereavement Room* podcast in response to her own experiences of feeling discriminated against within traditional bereavement support. Ali received negative comments from white members of her therapy training group when discussing the Muslim custom of prohibiting women from attending burials. Running to three seasons, *Bereavement Room* features a wealth of diaspora voices to understand the cultural, racial and religious nuances of grief, particularly while navigating largely white institutions and services. Ali's podcast pointed to the need for culturally sensitive bereavement support, such as the Mindful Muslims programme offered by community interest company the Delicate Mind. The brainchild of one of Ali's guests, Nikhwat Marawat, the Mindful Muslims programme offers peer-to-peer bereavement support for the Muslim community in Birmingham. Ali often attempted to raise important topics such as cultural sensitivity and institutional racism on Instagram, but felt she gained less traction than other accounts, largely run by white creators. After some time, she decided to fold her podcast and its Instagram page. When I ask her why, she talks not only about the lack of support she felt from the 'online grief community', but also about how her whole life became focused on grief. She felt she had become stuck in it and needed to move forward to protect her mental health.

I could understand how Ali felt stuck. During the pandemic, with little else to do, I would spend a lot of time on The Grief Network's Instagram page and regularly found myself emotionally exhausted. Since the Network only followed other grief accounts, the news feed was full of grief-related posts. Reading post after post reiterating how bad grief was had a cumulative effect. On top of this, the competitive statistics of Instagram, combined with the overwhelming number of messages we could receive in a day, made me feel like I was failing to provide enough support. Being stuck in a loop of grief content reaffirmed how negative and alienating it was to be bereaved but offered little means to feel the progress of growth. It was only when stepping away from the platform that I realised that unhealthy overuse was exactly what the app was designed to engender, predicated on anxieties about popularity and belonging. The echo chamber that social media creates is no different for the grief space. One account posting popular 'do and don't' tips for the friends of the bereaved announced that they were going to stop. They argued that, while those posts were the ones receiving the most engagement and affirmation from grieving people, they also found that many non-bereaved people were sending messages fretting about how to talk to their bereaved friend. In making so many non-bereaved people scared of getting things wrong, they were actually blocking important lines of communication.

*

Beyond the near future of social media, technology will impact how we grieve in the longer term by potentially altering our ongoing relationships with the deceased after they have died.

Today, you cannot 'be online' without leaving a digital footprint. Modern grief has begun to involve the need to deal with this online legacy. Carla Sofka, Professor of Social Work at Siena College, notes how opinion is divided on whether the social media profile of a dead person should become a place for memorial or not. Speaking on the *Social Work Podcast*, Sofka observes how dead people's social media profiles can become a target for trolls, or even identity theft. She suggests that hospice and social workers will increasingly need to assist grieving families with the digital admin of social media accounts and memorial pages as part of their roles.

As our data footprints become increasingly large, posthumous data management may become its own career. According to the Korea Employment Information Service, becoming a 'digital undertaker' was predicted to become a popular vocation in 2021, while the global death-care services market is estimated to grow to a $189.8 billion industry by 2030.[8] With a 2019 study from the Oxford Internet Institute at Oxford University finding that Facebook's dead users will outnumber living users by 2070, there is clearly such a need for digital undertaking.[9] Increasingly, the dying will be prompted to express their wishes about what happens with their 'digital remains' after death. For some, this may be to opt out of the digital sphere as far as possible, while others may choose instead to opt in to a digital afterlife. Already in gaming platforms like Animal Crossing or World of Warcraft, creating personal shrines to the deceased is a common practice. It is clear that the human instinct to grieve and memorialise will be expressed in whatever places we populate – even those that are online.

In the future, technology will enable us to do more than simple memorialisation. It will give us a more tangible relationship with the dead. In February 2021, Deep Nostalgia – a type of deepfake technology – went viral for its animation of photos and video clips of the dead. Old photographs are brought to life; the previously static individuals laugh, smile or raise their eyebrows. The effect reminds me of the magical photographs in *Harry Potter*, where the people depicted can move or even leave the frame altogether. Companies such as MyHeritage and GoodTrust are making this kind of magic a reality. Collaborating with D-ID, a deep-learning technology provider, both companies offer consumers a photo animation service, alongside other full-scale legacy management services such as online memory banks and vaults. In time, the data footprint left behind by the dead will be able to be harnessed by deep-learning and deepfake technology to create realistic, interactive avatars of them. Think of a more evolved version of the hologram of Kim Kardashian's dead father, which Kanye West 'gifted' his ex-wife on her fortieth birthday. When I asked other young grievers what they felt about West's hologram, reactions were mixed. Some said they'd love to see their person brought back to life, even if they knew it was fake. Others found the idea unsettling, or even disrespectful. Other ethical issues arise. Despite 81 per cent of people agreeing that society should take better care of the dead's digital legacy, according to GoodTrust,[10] since consumers don't own their own data, it is uncertain just by whom and how it will be used after they die. Edina Harbinja, a senior lecturer at Aston University, argues that people are currently at risk of 'digital grave robbers', who could hack anything from social media accounts and personal photos, to cryptocurrency wallets. 'In most countries in the world, the data of the deceased are not protected. So nothing in law would prevent the creation of an avatar or android that would resemble the dead.'[11]

Research carried out by the Oxford Internet Institute empha-sises the risk of dead people's data becoming a profitable asset for commercial platforms.[12] The researchers argued that the digital afterlife industry (DAI) must be regulated and harmo-nised in order to avoid exploitation of 'digital remains'. Professor Luciana Floridi comments: 'Human remains are not meant to be consumed by the morbidly curious. Regardless of whether they are the sole legal owner of the deceased's data – and irrespective of whether the opinion of their next of kin, with regulation, DAI firms would have to abide by certain conventions, such as preventing hate speech and the commer-cial exploitation of memorialised profiles.'

Still, in the future, users may opt in to the kind of afterlife technology enables, as products like Kanye's hologram will become increasingly more affordable. Paula Kiel, a PhD researcher at the London School of Economics, is exploring digital afterlives and the possibility for 'consciousness upload-ing' to bring comfort to grievers, as it may allow the bereaved to continue to interact, however artificially, with the person who has died. If we think about how stars who died in the analogue era, like Marilyn Monroe, have already been manipulated and commodified, it is easy to imagine the immense ethical issues that will surround the use of people's digital post-life consciences. Will such virtual immortality bring comfort to grievers or distort the grieving process? Will mishandling the deceased's data allow the exploitation of the dead for profit, advertising or entertainment?

I uploaded a photograph of my mother to GoodTrust's AI tool, curious to see how I would feel. I braced myself for her to come alive. The result was as I expected. The once-static image came to life: the corners of her mouth moved, her head seemed to shake and her eyebrows raised. It was life-like but clearly fake at the same time. It still made me burst into tears. Why is it different to rewatching old videos? Because it's new information. It is akin, I think, to finding an old photograph or video of the dead person that you didn't know you had. For a moment, the newness of that image or video allows your brain to process it as though that person is truly there – as though you're seeing them again for the first time in four, five, six years. I'm no scientist, but I imagine it lights up new neural pathways that don't fire when you look at an old photo that you are so intimately familiar with it doesn't do much to stir your emotions at all. I cried while gazing at my mother's face smiling back at me and saved the image. I immediately wanted to animate another photo, but when I clicked on the option, I was prompted to sign up to a subscription of $5 a month, giving me access to up to 10 animated photos. For a higher price, I could get more. I felt angry and cruelly reminded of my desperation.

Striving to create digital versions of the deceased is one step along the way of striving to beat death altogether. The wealthy are already able to pay hundreds and thousands to preserve their bodies at Alcor Life Extension Foundation, in California. The centre pauses the death process using cryogenics so that those preserved can come back to life once the technology exists. All this speaks to the strength of our impulse to prevent loss through death. It is, in my mind, no different from the reason that bereaved people will go to mediums in the hopes of communing with their dead person. In a new Disney+ show, *Extraordinary*, the 25-year-old protagonist Jen is able to talk to her dead father through her flatmate Carrie, who has the power to adopt the voice of the dead. In a number of scenes, Jen and

Carrie sit back to back, while Jen happily chats to her father's voice. I thought how wonderful that would be. Even if I could never see or be held by my mother again, to hear her voice and hear her thoughts and ask her advice would soothe so much of the pain. But how comfortable would that feel, knowing it was technology and not really her? And wouldn't using, or depending, on that technology open up yet more questions about whether you were grieving 'correctly'? On the other hand, how different is developing this technology to what our early ancestors have been doing all along? Memorialising the dead and conceiving of their afterlife, so better to keep their loved ones close and alive. Perhaps technology is, perversely, the vehicle through which we can reconnect with the inherent spirituality of human grief.

As uncomfortable as these questions feel now, our acclimatisation to new technology is moving at breakneck speed. We are quick to tell companies our private details in return for what they are selling or streaming. Taking a selfie was once deemed cringe-inducing and vain but is now such common practice we don't bat an eyelid. Even the idea of taking naked photos of ourselves would once have been anathema to most people but has become a worrying norm in dating among younger generations. The digital afterlife is just the next step in the technology that we will become accustomed to – something so pervasive, it will never cross our minds that, for thousands of years, we had no access to the dead beyond memories passed down orally through generations. Will digital afterlives take away the pain of grief? I don't think so. The fact that our loved one no longer lives or breathes – that we will never see them in bodily form or touch them again – will never not confound us. And I would query the impulse to try to 'fix' or 'solve' the pain of grief. As we know from our early ancestors, our ability to mourn and yearn for the dead is part of what makes us human.

*

Whether the way we grieve changes for the better or for the worse depends on how ready we, as a society, are to re-normalise death. Centres like Alcor suggest we are moving further away from readily accepting that death is a part of life. In recent years, however, a strong countermovement has sought to re-educate society on death, encouraging people to embrace death positivity. Opening up conversations about death can only help open up conversations about grief in turn.

Kathryn Mannix, in her book *With the End in Mind: Dying, Death and Wisdom in an Age of Denial*, details what a 'normal' death looks like. Mannix worked as a palliative care consultant and pioneered cognitive behavioural therapy (CBT) for the terminally ill, to help improve their quality of life in the lead-up to death. She makes a similar point about death as I do about grief. When all we learn about death is the dramatic, grisly endings we see on the television, we are horribly ill-prepared for the real thing, either when facing death ourselves or facing the death of someone close. When my mother stated that she wished to stay at home after she died, before the funeral, I was disturbed by the idea of having a dead body in the house. It was, in fact, a positive experience as it allowed me time to realise my mother was no longer living. I was only able to handle her death and the immediate aftermath because I had been properly prepared by the undertakers about the process of dying and the changes that happen to a dead body.

Mannix advocates for far greater death literacy, to reduce the fear and repression that currently surround us when it comes to thinking about 'the end': 'The sensationalised yet simultaneously trivialised versions of dying and death [we see on television, in novels and in the news] have replaced what was once everyone's common experience of observing the dying of people around them, of seeing death often enough to recognise its patterns, to become familiar with life lived well within the limits of decreasing vigour, and even to develop a familiarity with the sequences of the deathbed.' As medicine and healthcare improved in the latter half of the twentieth century, our hopes of being cured have, too. But for those who cannot be cured, the rush to hospital and rounds of treatments often replace a calmer death at home. 'Instead of dying in a dear and familiar room with people we love around us, we now die in ambulances and emergency rooms and intensive care units, our loved ones separated from us by the machinery of life preservation.' Mannix tells us that death follows recognisable patterns similar to birth, with the irony that death is often less painful than the latter, despite the stereotypes of agony and indignity we are now accustomed to. Being familiar with the patterns of death is comforting, as I know from first-hand experience. I was reassured that my mother was not in pain and it gave me the strength to stay in the room and be by her side as she died. I wouldn't have had it any other way.

The pandemic forced death back onto centre stage in a way that many of us may never have experienced before. Only those who lived through and were directly affected by the AIDS crisis of the 1980s will have experienced something similar in their lifetimes. In the early days of the pandemic, it was a reminder that we humans – so confident in our innovations and technology – are still powerless against something so microscopic and novel. Death loomed large and, with it, fear. Harrowing stories of lonely and painful deaths will not have done much to foster the education and knowledge-is-power approach that those like Mannix advocate.

There are also signs, however, that the pandemic may well have accelerated the death positivity trend, particularly among the younger generation. According to the UK will-writing start-up Farewill, more Millennials considered writing their own will than before the pandemic. In April 2020, at the peak of the pandemic in the UK, the company reported that the number of under-35s writing their own wills was 12 times higher than in 2019. Meanwhile, the start-up Aura, which aims to enable the terminally ill to leave a legacy for loved ones, found that Gen Z were the demographic who had the most open and mature outlook on death, being four times more likely than Baby Boomers to plan ahead and make bucket lists for their life. They were also over four times more likely to speak to their families about death, perhaps spurred on by the wider availability of information online and on social media.

Indeed, death is also getting a makeover. Design studio the Liminal Space created Life Support, a digital platform aiming to help open up conversation about loss and grief, noting that a third of people think about death or dying at least once a week, while Exit Here is a contemporary funeral parlour offering very modern planning and hospitality services along-side design-led caskets and urns. It is the brainchild of restaurateur Oliver Peyton, who established the Chiswick location after planning the funerals of his own parents. 'We don't use a lot of black. We try to make things a little more joyous, but the main thing we do is give people choice.' One of the rationales behind the distinct aesthetic of Exit Here is to refocus the industry on celebrating life and breaking down taboos, so that people have a say in how they want to be remembered and celebrated.

Choice is perhaps the key. One of my mother's few rules for her funeral was 'no black'. We chose a funeral director who enabled 'bespoke' funerals, meaning my mother was buried in a white wicker casket bearing her favourite flowers and no one was wearing funereal clothes and no hymns were sung. It was a comfort that she had had a hand in planning everything, and our conversations about it helped to make her funeral something that I was engaged in, rather than the strange and alienating affair many young people I spoke to reported, feeling almost as if they had been transported inside a stereotype that made it difficult to believe it was really *their* person that they were burying. These tried-and-true traditions are not even so old themselves, hailing from the Victorian era when funeral directors only had a role in providing coffins and transporting the body. It is within the twentieth century that undertakers' roles grew to becoming the caretaker of the body, the embalming and the funeral as an event. Many businesses have been passed down through families and the lack of innovation on the 'mainstream' level has led to an investigation of the industry from the Competition & Markets Authority. Key recommendations from the report published in December 2020 included an obligation to disclose prices for ease of comparison, a prohibition on commercial interests such as incentives from hospitals and care homes, and a broader regulatory regime to monitor the quality of services provided.[13] When couched in these terms, it is clear why many people are now seeking to opt for something alternative and more personalised.

Though it may not be obvious, funerals have been as impacted by technology as other areas of our lives. Post-mortem photos – photos of the recently deceased, common in the Victorian era – emerged when commercial photography became readily available in the 1830s and were popular until the turn of the century. Cremation, too, was considered a more unusual alternative to burial, but now 75 per cent of people are cremated in the UK, and 78.8 per cent are forecast to be cremated in America by 2035, according to the National Funeral Directors Association.[14] Just as those bereaved during the First World War had to conceive of new ways of memorialising dead soldiers who could not be repatriated, society was forced to innovate during the pandemic. With funerals kept very small or prohibited entirely, many people were unable to be by the bedside of the dying or to attend their funeral. FaceTime good-byes and Zoom funerals became the new norm. Online funerals, or hybrid funerals, met the sudden need for people to be 'there' in the ritual, even if they could not be there physically. Speaking to Hope Edelman, she tells me she hopes it continues. 'Of course, it's better to be there in person. But for people who can't travel or can't take the time off work, feeling that they are able to attend in some way is helpful in processing grief.'

In today's climate-conscious world, one major innovation is the sustainable burial. In Seattle, Recompose is a centre offering an alternative to burial and cremation through human compost-ing, following the legalisation of the practice in Washington in 2018. The state of California recently also legalised composting, which consists of placing human remains in reusable steel vessels with other biodegradable materials like wood chips to decompose for just over a month. In Paris, the Ivry-sur-Seine green burial area is designed to reduce the carbon emissions typically generated by traditional burials, with the plot welcoming only cardboard or unvarnished wood coffins and urns, while the dead must be dressed only in natural fibres. Headstones will be replaced by plain wooden grave markers. And in the Netherlands, the 'Living Cocoon' mycelium coffin, which takes a week to grow using local waste products that are absorbed back into nature within a month, is covered by the largest insurer in the country. Currently, the UK's Law Commission is reviewing old laws on the disposal of the deceased, citing the fact that many are outdated and the deceased has no enshrined right for their wishes around burial to be respected. The current laws also only contemplate burial and cremation, and the review will aim to update the law to ensure alternative methods of disposal can legally be accommodated.

Beyond sustainability, you may also be able to 3D print your coffin in a bid to circumvent regulations around euthanasia. Radical pro-euthanasia campaigner Dr Philip Nitschke has designed a 3D-printed self-killing machine made of biodegradable materials. The contraption delivers a peaceful death when you enter, at the time of your choosing, making it possible for you to attend your own funeral, perhaps stepping inside as the finale of your own end-of-life party. There is clearly an ethical debate to be had around a euthanasia machine. But think back to the medieval European conception of a good death: one that happens in public, where you are surrounded by your community, your priest and your family, and fully prepared for the next step. Is an end-of-life party so different?

Living funerals – where a terminally ill person throws their own end-of-life celebration ahead of their death – are becoming more common, even now. Golden Charter, one of the UK's biggest funeral-plan providers, reports that living funerals began in Japan in the mid-nineties, where they are known as *seizensō*. The trend developed to allow elders to feel that they were unburdening younger generations from the stress of a classic funeral. They remain popular in the country, are now common in the US, and are beginning to be seen in the UK. Writing in the *i*, the celebrant Amanda Waring says that the possibility that such events give for a terminally ill person to talk about their life and for their relatives and friends to tell them what they are grateful for can help all involved in accepting the death and processing their grief.[15]

Reframing the conversation around death – or, more aptly, re*opening* it – not only helps those who know their lives are going to end, but also those who are left behind. Of course, not all of us know we are about to die, and those bereaved after a sudden death do not have the same opportunity to have the conversations that the anticipatorily bereaved do. But there is no reason not to have those conversations when we are not expecting death. Logistically, ensuring that as much death admin is done and up to date as possible also helps those bereaved. The UK Bereavement Commission emphasised the difficulties the newly bereaved face in attempting to close bank accounts, change bills into a new name and shut down social media accounts. Making sure those close to you know what your wishes are and where to find everything if you were to die helps ease the burden on those left behind.

Soon after I finished reading Kathryn Mannix's book, I was asked to appear on a new podcast called *Deathbed Discs*, hosted by Jade de Robles Rossdale. I was asked to talk about the five songs I would like to be played at my funeral and why. Thinking through my choices and imagining what I might like my funeral to be like was oddly comforting. While contemplating death often feels fearful, thinking about how you would like to be sent off and how you would like to be remembered offers the opportunity to reflect on your life and your wishes. It allowed me to regain a sense of perspective – even one of love and gratitude.

Young bereaved people in particular can spend decades anticipating their own untimely deaths, at the very age that the people they lost died. At 30 I now feel a sense of urgency that I don't believe is related entirely to the normal pressures placed on people at my age. My mother died in her early sixties; by the time she was 31 she had lived half her life, though she didn't know it. Though I don't articulate it, even to myself most days, I know I expect not to live to old age. I expect to get cancer. Sitting and thinking about what I might want at that time, who I might be, who might come to my funeral, and acknowledging that even if I only have 30 years left, I'm sure my life will still be astronomically different to what it is now, helps that death anxiety.

*

So why, in 2018, did the support I was looking for not exist? Well, history now tells me that the answer is quite simple. Bereavement support in the West is a relatively new phenomenon, because we didn't always need it. Informal support through the community, alongside a greater expectation and acceptance of death, made grief a common part of life. Bereavement support developed in response to the socially traumatic move in the last century from collective modes of grieving to private mourning behind closed doors. The best-known bereavement charity, Cruse Bereavement Care, was founded in 1959, originally as a support group for widows and their families. Winston's Wish, the first bereavement charity for children in the UK, was founded in the year I was born – 1992. Child Bereavement UK came just a couple of years later in 1994. Hope Edelman tells me that when she lost her mother, in Reagan's America in 1981, there was no hospice or charity to turn to. In the grand scale of human history – and therefore in the evolution of how humans grieve – support in this format is essentially still a cutting-edge innovation. It has simply failed to keep up with the speed of wider social developments.

When my mother died, I took it for granted that a group tailored to twenty-somethings would exist. Yet, given that support tailored to children didn't come into existence until the decade I was born, it's no wonder that emerging adults – a demographic that didn't have a name until the turn of the millennium – would still be almost entirely underserved and unrecognised in that space. Looking through the available studies, it appears that emerging adults have only been treated as a distinct demographic within grief research in the past few years, with many papers only dating back to the mid-2010s. In this respect, I see The Grief Network and other groups like it as being at the forefront of a continuing evolution of our understanding of grief. Recognising that emerging adults (and other diverse demographics) face specific challenges is part of a greater reckoning society must have with our cultural grief inheritance.

So what is to come in the future? If we need a model for how to evolve bereavement support in helpful ways, we can look to our distant past. We must re-socialise grief and bring it back into the public arena, the way that online grief creators are currently doing. We must ensure that technology treats our loved ones' remains and memories ethically, so they are harnessed to enable a continuing bond with the dead, rather than disrespect their memory. And we must get comfortable again with death and finality. In so doing, we might just find it easier to live.

Epilogue

The day my mother died, the season changed overnight. March had been freakishly cold, bringing snow both to Berlin and London. When she died in the early hours of that mid-April morning, the dawn brought soft, warm sunlight. Daffodils – her favourite flowers – seemed to have sprung up overnight. When I went for a walk with my friend up the hill near my house, I hated the irony of it. Spring, with all its revenant imagery, its suggestion of hope and resurrection. Still, taking in that pristine day, I couldn't help but be moved by a strange sense of hope – something that verged even on delirious joy. Because I had *had* her. In that moment, it felt like 25 years with her – 25 years of her love – was enough to sustain me for a lifetime.

As I come to finish writing this book, spring is in sight once again. Every year it takes me by surprise because I am so busy enduring the winter. I am always happy to feel the change in season; it brings lighter mornings and the stirring of life. It feels, to me, like when the new year truly begins. The shift in season also tells my body I am fast approaching that one-two punch of my birthday, and the anniversary of my mother's death the following day. It takes me back to memories of that day and the hard months leading up to it. This year, it will be five years since my mother died. I will turn 31.

My life has changed almost entirely since I was that 25-year-old, hungover on the couch in Bath the day after finishing my master's finals, unaware that I was about to hear news that would alter my life completely. In the space of the last year alone, I have started dating someone new, I got a kitten, I bought a flat, I finished a degree, I started a new job, I wrote a book, I turned 30. The changes I made all stemmed from decisions I took in the depths of the coronavirus lockdown. Realising that my twenties were effectively over (I knew I would be 30 by the time lockdown was lifted), I decided I needed to get my life on solid ground and start building for the future I'd always found so hard to imagine. I'd never thought about what I wanted from life in my thirties, or forties, or fifties, firstly because I was so busy *being in my twenties* (and thinking about what that should look like) that I never thought much beyond them, and secondly, because when Mum died, I couldn't picture what the future could look like anyway.

Change has been exciting, but it has also been painful. It has taken me further and further away from the version of myself that my mother last knew. Though I know she would have encouraged it all, and remembering old advice of hers has inspired me to take new leaps of faith, the fact that I cannot share the successes I have worked hard for is tough. I have found myself, for the first time since my mother was dying, awake at night racked with sobs, crying hard because I can't believe she's really gone. At nearly five years since her death, grief has felt more painful than it ever has before. I am a long way from those soft, slim edges of joy and gratitude that I felt, unbelievably, on the day my mother died.

There are things I know I wrote or felt or expressed much closer to the time of my mother's death that were more hopeful, resilient and life-affirming than anything I have felt recently. 'Pain is the agent of change' is a phrase of Julia Samuel's that swirls around in my head sometimes when I let the tears course through my chest late at night. It is mixed in there with a vague curiosity as to whether my neighbour upstairs hears these wails, and the faint worry that I will never stop feeling this much pain and that life will always feel 'lesser' than it did before. Even though I have been told time and again that grief will never go away, I still catch myself wondering the same thing. Will this ever stop? When will this get better? When will I just be OK about this?

It is customary to end a book like this on a note of hope. I resist, because now is not a moment in which I find my relationship with my grief to be one that feels very hopeful. The hope is in the pain. Though my grief has been disruptive in the past year, I have often felt happy that it is moving me because I feel closer to my mum for it. I feel closer to her memory because I am reaching out to try to intuit what she might say or how she might feel about what I am doing with my adulthood, now that I feel I am finally stepping into it. The pain is reassuring, because for some years after her death, when I was *doing* so much with my grief, I would sit in quiet moments and realise I didn't actually feel her there. I spent so much time advocating that we talk about grief, I found I had distracted myself from really sitting with mine. I am coming to a moment in life when I need to practise what I preach. I have seen so much change in bereavement support in the past few years, I feel confident that momentum can only build. It might be time to pass on the baton and allow myself a moment to breathe, and to grieve.

The hope is also found in knowing I won't always feel this way. When you tell a story, you expect it to end. But grief doesn't end. The feeling of joy on the morning of my mother's death, the feeling of loneliness and yearning five years later – these are not a beginning and an end, but two waypoints in a long process, in a story that will never be complete, nor ever fully told. Neither is representative of what grief is, or was, or will be. Every quarter-life griever interviewed for this book provided their own snapshot of grief, one that might only have been accurate or true in the moment I spoke to them but could have become inaccurate even hours after hanging up the call. If I interviewed all of them again tomorrow, or in a year or a decade, their grief would have taken on a different shape. They would have come up against different edges, feelings or memories. Just like me, their grief will be there on any given day, doing its imperceptible tidal thing of ebbing and flowing, sometimes out of sight, sometimes rising to the surface when least expected. It always will be, even after you turn the last page.

Acknowledgements

First and foremost, my thanks to everyone who gave up their time to speak to me for this book. Your various insights, memories and experiences will go a long way in helping those who have picked it up in hopes of feeling less alone. Thank you for trusting me with your stories and, in doing so, encouraging other people to tell theirs. Thank you to the experts and psychologists who helped inform this book, in particular Julia Samuel and Hope Edelman, to whom this book is indebted. Your insights have and continue to change my life and my relationship with grief.

A special thanks to Bonnie, Katie, Fi, Katy, Beccy, Jess and Hannah. I wouldn't have had the emotional capacity to run a first Grief Network meet-up without your help, let alone make TGN what it became. Thank you for replying to my lonely little podcast letter and dedicating so much of your time and emotional energy to forging a space for other young people going through the same thing. Your ideas and commitment sparked magic and you helped to create something pretty special and unforgettable. Thank you also for helping me make (my) grief sometimes kind of … fun.

Thank you to my brilliant agent Lisette, for seeing something in the slim skeleton of a book I sent when I was just a baby writer of 26 years old and helping me to grow as an author. Even when there were disappointments, you never stopped believing in my talent as a writer and helped me to keep developing and keep drafting. I know this book has personal resonance for you and your siblings; thank you for continuing to work on it, even when I know it can't have been an easy choice.

Thank you to Jo and the team at William Collins for your hard work in bringing this book to life. You immediately 'got' my pitch and what I wanted to do with this story; you could see that grief can be examined beyond the personal and is a topic that deserves wide-ranging enquiry. Thank you for contending with all the other demands on my time and getting the text into a better shape than I thought I had the capacity to achieve. It is a better text for your thoughtful edits and feedback.

To all my friends who have supported me throughout these tumultuous years: Bridget, Bella, Tilly, Alex, Melissa, Georgia, Sydney, Lauren K-J, Lauren M, Jo, Adam, Alexi and Katie, Sophie, Jess, Felix. To Nicky, my sweet and sensitive Pisces, for being by my side in my darkest moments. To Harriet, for always knowing how to cheer me up (with garlic bread and chocolate), thank you for being my most avid reader, supporter, and always having my back. To Lewis, for being the sweetest soul I know and making me laugh even when I'm crying. Honourable mention to the entire Mitchell clan who support and celebrate me from the other side of the globe. To Henry, Ella and George – I am so lucky that I was put in Group A with you.

To Stephen, my cornerman and (sometimes) cheerleader. You encouraged me to keep going with this book and all the other endeavours even when I was overwhelmed and wanted to give up. You remind me to (strive to) be excellent even when I am feeling decidedly 'fml'. You have dedicated so much of your time, love and energy to me as I navigated Spaghetti Junction, and you have taken care of me in the most basic sense even when I didn't have the energy to take care of myself. Thank you for backing me. I love the special and tender memories we have made together, and I love our beautiful, blended pud family. I love you, dearly.

To James and Dad for supporting me and for keeping Mum's memory alive. I love you. And finally, to Mum. It is strange to want to show you this book because it wouldn't exist if you were still here. I often struggled to write it for that very reason. You taught me everything I know about compassion and resilience, but I would swap all those lessons in a fraction of a heartbeat if I could give you another hug. Thank you for everything. I love you.

Notes

Chapter One: *Quarter-life Grief*

1. Jeffrey Arnett, 'Emerging Adulthood: A Theory of Development from the Late Teens Through the Twenties', *American Psychologist*, 55:5 (May 2000), 469–480.
2. Jeffrey Arnett et al., 'The new life stage of emerging adulthood at ages 18–29 years: implications for mental health', *Lancet Psychiatry*, 1:7 (December 2014), 569–76: https://pubmed.ncbi.nlm.nih.gov/26361316/
3. Jeffrey Arnett, 'Emerging Adulthood: What Is It, and What Is It Good For?' *Child Development Perspectives*, 1:2 (2007), 68–73.
4. Jeffrey Arnett, 'Emerging Adulthood: A Theory of Development from the Late Teens Through the Twenties', *American Psychologist*, 55:5 (May 2000), 471.
5. Danielle Sinay, 'Gen Z doesn't want to get married as younger generations re-define "monogamy"', *indy100* (30 August 2021): https://www.indy100.com/lifestyle/gen-z-millennial-marriage-monogamy-relationships-b1910213

6. Christine Michel Carter, 'Gen Z Women Postpone Motherhood Because of the Challenges Working Millennial Moms Encounter', *Forbes* (20 June 2022): https://www.forbes.com/sites/christinecarter/2022/06/20/gen-z-women-postpone-motherhood-because-of-the-challenges-working-millennial-moms-encounter/

7. Robert Booth, 'Happiness among UK young people has hit 13-year low, study finds', *Guardian* (23 February 2022): https://www.theguardian.com/society/2022/feb/23/happiness-among-uk-young-people-has-hit-13-year-low-study-finds

8. 'UK death and bereavement statistics', Child Bereavement UK: https://www.childbereavementuk.org/death-bereavement-statistics

9. Robert Neimeyer et al., 'Lessons of loss: Meaning-making in bereaved college students', *New Directions for Student Services*, 121 (February 2008), 27–39.

10. Natalie Porter and Amy Claridge, 'Unique grief experiences: The needs of emerging adults facing the death of a parent', *Death Studies*, 45:3 (2021) 191–201.

11. Sara Newcomb-Anjo et al., 'A Person-Centered Analysis of Risk Factors That Compromise Wellbeing in Emerging Adulthood', *Journal of Youth and Adolescence*, 46 (2017), 867–883.

12. Shannen Jones and Matteo Martini, 'Sense of self, depression and adaption to grief, in emerging adults who suffered parental loss', *Current Psychology* (22 May 2021): https://link.springer.com/article/10.1007/s12144-021-01843-z

13. Natalie Porter and Amy Claridge, 'Unique grief experiences: The needs of emerging adults facing the death of a parent', *Death Studies*, 45:3 (2021), 191–201.

Chapter Two: *Leavers*

1. M. Stroebe and H. Schut, 'The dual process model of coping with bereavement: rationale and description', *Death Studies*, 23:3 (April–May 1999), 197–224.

2. 'Alcohol Consumption UK', Drink Aware: https://www.drinkaware.co.uk/research/alcohol-facts-and-data/alcohol-consumption-uk#howmanypeopledonotdrinkalcohol

3. University of Michigan, 'More young adults are abstaining from alcohol', ScienceDaily (12 October 2020): https://www.sciencedaily.com/releases/2020/10/201012120007.htm

4. Megan Brenan, 'U.S. Alcohol Consumption on Low End of Recent Readings', Gallup (19 August 2021): https://news.gallup.com/poll/353858/alcohol-consumption-low-end-recent-readings.aspx

5. John Holmes et al., 'Youth drinking in decline: What are the implications for public health, public policy and public debate?', *International Journal on Drug Policy*, 102:103606 (April 2022): https://www.ncbi.nlm.nih.gov/pmc/articles/PMC7612362/

6. Johanna Gerhold, 'New market, new rules: How Gen Z's are changing the alcohol industry', Think with Google (May 2019): https://www.thinkwithgoogle.com/intl/en-gb/future-of-marketing/management-and-culture/diversity-and-inclusion/new-market-new-rules-how-genzs-are-changing-alcohol-industry/

7. Adam Burgess et al., '"More options … less time" in the "hustle culture" of "generation sensible": Individualization and drinking decline among twenty-first century young adults', *British Journal of Sociology*, 73:4 (September 2022), 903–918.

8. Johanna Gerhold, 'New market, new rules: How Gen Z's are changing the alcohol industry', Think with Google (May 2019): https://www.thinkwithgoogle.com/intl/en-gb/future-of-marketing/management-and-culture/diversity-and-inclusion/new-market-new-rules-how-genzs-are-changing-alcohol-industry/

Chapter Four: *Dream Jobs*

1. Robert Van Giezen, 'Paid leave in private industry over the past 20 years', *Beyond the Numbers*, 2:18 (August 2013): https://www.bls.gov/opub/btn/volume-2/paid-leave-in-private-industry-over-the-past-20-years.htm

2. UK Commission on Bereavement, 'Bereavement is everyone's business', 2022 Report: https://bereavementcommission.org.uk/media/jaqex1t5/bereavement-is-everyone-s-business-full-report_1.pdf

3. Stephen Moeller, 'Grief in the Workplace', Grief Recovery Method (7 July 2017): https://www.griefrecoverymethod.com/blog/2017/07/grief-workplace

4. 'Sue Ryder calls for statutory paid bereavement leave', Sue Ryder (9 November 2020): https://www.sueryder.org/news/sue-ryder-calls-for-statutory-paid-bereavement-leave

5. Lionel Standing et al., 'Exceptional achievement and early parental loss: the Phaeton effect in American writers, presidents, and eminent individuals', *Journal of Psychohistory*, 42:3 (2015), 188–99.

6. Rachel Sylvester and Alice Thomson, *What I Wish I'd Known When I Was Young: The Art and Science of Growing Up* (William Collins, 2022).

Chapter Five: *All My Friends*

1. Connor Ibbetson, 'Who are the most lonely people in the UK?', YouGov (3 October 2019): https://yougov.co.uk/topics/society/articles-reports/2019/10/03/young-britons-are-most-lonely

2. Colleen Walsh, 'Young adults hardest hit by loneliness during pandemic', *Harvard Gazette* (17 February 2021): https://news.harvard.edu/gazette/story/2021/02/young-adults-teens-loneliness-mental-health-coronavirus-covid-pandemic/

3. 'Protecting Youth Mental Health: The U.S. Surgeon General's Advisory' (2021): https://www.hhs.gov/sites/default/files/surgeon-general-youth-mental-health-advisory.pdf

4. Manuela Barreto et al., 'Loneliness around the world: Age, gender, and cultural differences in loneliness', *Personality and Individual Differences*, 169 (1 February 2021), 110066: https://www.sciencedirect.com/science/article/pii/S0191886920302555

5. 'Protecting Youth Mental Health: The U.S. Surgeon General's Advisory' (2021): https://www.hhs.gov/sites/default/files/surgeon-general-youth-mental-health-advisory.pdf

6. UK Commission on Bereavement, 'Bereavement is everyone's business', 2022 Report: https://bereavementcommission.org.uk/media/jaqex1t5/bereavement-is-everyone-s-business-full-report_1.pdf

Chapter Six: *Marriage and Children*

1. Cynthia Pill and Judith Zabin, 'Lifelong Legacy of Early Maternal Loss: A Women's Group', *Clinical Social Work Journal*, 25 (1997), 179–95. See also, Hope Edelman, *Motherless Mothers: How Losing a Mother Shapes the Parent You Become* (HarperPerennial, 2007).

2. Wendy Mitchell and Eileen Green, '"I Don't Know What I'd Do Without Our Mam": Motherhood, Identity and Support Networks', *Sociological Review*, 50:1 (2002), 1–22.

3. Bronwyn Harman, 'Motherless Mothers: Maternally Bereaved Women in Their Everyday Roles as Mothers', *Journal of Family Studies*, 20:1 (June 2014) 28.

Chapter Seven: *Future Grief*

1. Nicholas Quah, 'We're Entering the Era of Big Podcasting', *Vulture* (30 September 2019): https://www.vulture.com/ 2019/09/podcasting-history-three-eras.html

2. 'Estimated number of podcast listeners in the United Kingdom (UK) from 2017 to 2026', Statista (7 February 2022): https:// www.statista.com/forecasts/1147560/podcast-reach-uk

3. Susannah Goldsbrough, '*The High Low* podcast soundtracked the lives of thousands of women – we will miss it sorely', *The Telegraph* (2 December 2020): https://www.telegraph.co.uk/ radio/what-to-listen-to/high-low-podcast-soundtracked-lives-thousands-women-will-miss/#:~:text=In%20just%20over%20 150%20episodes,culture%20and%20female%20friendship%20 alike

4. 'Gartner Says Marketers Must Focus on Boosting Gen Z's Personal Brand to Make Them Loyal Customers', Business Wire (22 May 2019): https://www.businesswire.com/news/ home/20190522005069/en/Gartner-Says-Marketers-Must-Focus-on-Boosting-Gen-Z%E2%80%99s-Personal-Brand-to-Make-Them-Loyal-Customers

5. UK Commission on Bereavement, 'Bereavement is everyone's business', 2022 Report: https://bereavementcommission.org. uk/media/jaqex1t5/bereavement-is-everyone-s-business-full-report_1.pdf

6. Ibid.

7. Jessica Lindsay, 'The problem with mental health influencers', *Metro* (9 May 2021): https://metro.co.uk/2021/05/09/mental-health-influencers-providing-vital-support-or-hoodwinking-the-vulnerable-14381681/

8. 'Global Death Care Services Industry' market report, Global Industry Analysts (January 2023): https://www.reportlinker. com/p05960605/Global-Death-Care-Services-Industry. html?utm_source=GNW

9. Carl J. Öhman and David Watson, 'Are the dead taking over Facebook? A Big Data approach to the future of death online', *Big Data & Society*, 6:1 (2019): https://journals.sagepub.com/doi/10.1177/2053951719842540

10. 'Survey: Most Americans Unprepared With Their Real Life And Digital One', GoodTrust (28 March 2011): https://mygoodtrust.com/articles/survey-most-americans-unprepared-digital-life-real-one

11. Joanna England, 'Microsoft patents chatbot for "talking to dead people"', *Mobile* (7 January 2021): https://mobile-magazine.com/technology-and-ai/microsoft-patents-chatbot-talking-dead-people

12. 'Digital remains should be treated like physical ones', University of Oxford (18 April 2018): https://www.ox.ac.uk/news/2018-04-18-digital-remains-should-be-treated-physical-ones

13. Funerals market study by Competition & Markets Authority, Gov.UK (1 June 2018): https://www.gov.uk/cma-cases/funerals-market-study#final-report

14. 'Cremation on the Rise: NFDA Predicts the National Cremation Rate Will Climb by a Third Within 20 Years', National Funeral Directors Association (12 July 2018): https://nfda.org/news/media-center/nfda-news-releases/id/3526/cremation-on-the-rise-nfda-predicts-the-national-cremation-rate-will-climb-by-a-third-within-20-years

15. Amanda Waring, 'Why more and more people are attending their own funeral', *iNews* (25 May 2019): https://inews.co.uk/opinion/living-funerals-eco-funerals-amanda-waring-295260